CANADA
IN THE
BALANCE

CANADA IN THE BALANCE

BOB RAE

100

McCLELLAND & STEWART

Library and Archives Canada Cataloguing in Publication

Rae, Bob, 1948–
Canada in the balance / Bob Rae.

ISBN-13: 978-0-7710-7285-7
ISBN-10: 0-7710-7285-6

1. Canada–Social policy. 2. Canada–Economic policy–21st century.
3. Canada–Politics and government–21st century. 4. Political
planning–Canada. I. Title.

FC635.R327 2006   320.60971'09051   c2006-903419-2

We acknowledge the financial support of the Government of Canada
through the Book Publishing Industry Development Program and
that of the Government of Ontario through the Ontario Media
Development Corporation's Ontario Book Initiative. We further
acknowledge the support of the Canada Council for the Arts and the
Ontario Arts Council for our publishing program.

Typeset in Bell by M&S, Toronto
Printed and bound in Canada

This book is printed on acid-free paper that is 100% recycled,
ancient-forest friendly (100% post-consumer recycled).

McClelland & Stewart Ltd.
75 Sherbourne Street
Toronto, Ontario
M5A 2P9
www.mcclelland.com

1 2 3 4 5   10 09 08 07 06

For *Arlene, Judith, Lisa, and Eleanor,*
"once more into the breach"

CONTENTS

INTRODUCTION

I write these words in the early morning at my family cottage in eastern Ontario. It is a cool, grey spring day, with only the waking birds breaking the silence. I am fifty-seven and in good health. Why run again for public office? Why as a Liberal?

From a selfish standpoint I can see a future of, say, a few decades ahead. Having lost my dear brother David to cancer, I also know that there is no predicting the future. But to talk of the next twenty-five years is to talk of a world I hope to see. The next fifty years is the world of my three daughters, now in their twenties. Beyond that, the world of my grandchildren, the next generation.

I once heard a South African judge describe his country as "the world in one place": A small but powerful, rich world. A large, and growing, poor one. A world of stark contrasts, of conflicts, but also one of achievement and hope. Few could have predicted that the extraordinary leadership of one man, Nelson Mandela, could have contributed so dramatically to a peaceful transition to democracy and the rule of law. Canadians also often describe ourselves as "the world in one country." We are now a decidedly multicultural and multinational place. Unlike South Africa, we are as a whole far better off than the world average. But there is enough poverty – on Aboriginal reserves, in our inner cities and suburbs, in parts of rural Canada – to make us less affluent than some would like to think.

"We are the world" also has a deeper meaning. The borders and boundaries between countries are coming down. A company's supply chain extends across the globe. The phrase *national economy* has much less meaning than it once did and *global economy* much more. The dramatic change in places like India and China, where economies grow at an exceptionally fast pace, and where technology and communication are instantly linking people and businesses to the wider world, are no longer concerns of a few. Whether we call the world shrinking or flat, the point is the same: there is no escaping interdependence.

In the next quarter-century, Canada's population will be enriched by millions more people from around the globe making this country their home. Our wealth will be even more dependent not only on our internal strength, but also on trade and investment with the rest of the world.

Climate change is also quite literally a global phenomenon. The industrialization of the world leads to more greenhouse emissions, which lead inexorably to change in the Earth's atmosphere, which in turn is increasing the temperature of the planet. Oceans will rise, weather will become more extreme; more people will die from tornadoes, hurricanes, and flooding. Even deeper disasters – a dramatic change in the Gulf Stream, a massive reduction of the rain forest – are, we are told, possible.

Politically we are brought together as well. Insecurity in one part of the world can readily lead to violence somewhere else. A world whose populations in the Middle East, in Africa, in Asia continue to grow at a rapid pace faces human challenges on a scale that will require all of our ingenuity to meet. Put another way: Always ask yourself, What percentage of a population is under the age of eighteen? And then ask, What is the rate of employment? The answers to these questions tell us what people face for the future. They make us realize the extent of the challenge.

It all comes down to people: Villages where young women and men die of AIDS because there is no money for medicine. Five thousand children a day dying – from malaria, from starvation, from AIDS – when it is actually extreme and entirely predictable poverty that is killing them. This, too, is our world.

Canada and Canadians are caught up in this world. On First Nations reserves today, most of the population is under the age of eighteen. When those children have access to the Internet and television, they see a very different world from the one immediately around them. Many will leave their homes for jobs or school, heading to cities or towns and uncertain futures. Will they find a welcoming place, a place that respects them, treats them with dignity? Will they find the education they need? Will they find work? Will they find the chance to make their way in the world?

The next twenty-five years will tell a story. Canada can play a meaningful role in ending extreme poverty in the world. It can provide an exciting range of opportunities for all its citizens. It can become a leader in reducing pollution and in slowing climate change. It can help open up the world for its entrepreneurs. It can ensure that we are more prosperous and that opportunities are deeply and widely shared. Canada can also play a role in reducing insecurity and violence in the world.

Whether this happens depends on choices we make today. This book is about these choices and how they will inevitably affect the future. But we should all be asking ourselves these questions: What do we see on the horizon? What sort of country and world do we aspire to for our children, our grandchildren, and ourselves? And how best can we get there?

I have many people to thank for helping me to get this book written in the midst of a busy time. My assistant, Cynthia Diamond, helped throughout and I thank her most warmly. My friends Paul Genest, Jonathan Goldbloom, Gene Lang, and Priscilla Mouzakiotis were generous with their time and opinions. Judith Maxwell, Martha Friendly, Jonathan Hausman, and many others advised on social and economic issues. Louise Comeau and Stewart Elgie were especially helpful on environmental matters. Janice Stein and David Cameron have counselled me extensively on foreign policy and constitutional issues. Many political colleagues have helped as well.

My wife, Arlene Perly Rae, and our three daughters, Judith, Lisa, and Eleanor, have assisted me with research, debating ideas, and keeping perspective. This book is dedicated to them with much gratitude and love.

The Last Ten Years:
Some Lessons Learned

I HAVE WRITTEN ABOUT MY EARLIER POLITICAL career in two books, *From Protest to Power* and *The Three Questions.* Since they are both available to the reader, I will not repeat that narrative here.

The decade since 1996 has been very much a second career, beginning with my association with the Goodmans law firm in Toronto. To return to the practice of law with such a congenial and able group of colleagues has been a real pleasure. My work on corporate governance and restructuring has taken me into the practical and ever-changing world of the marketplace. I have developed an even deeper conviction that how a society becomes and remains prosperous lies at the heart of successful public policy.

In a great many countries, this question has been seized as a central one by reforming social democratic parties. Despite the best efforts of a few, such has not been the case with Canada's federal New Democratic Party (NDP). I resigned from the NDP when I was named to the Security Intelligence Review Committee (SIRC) by Prime Minister Jean Chrétien in 1998. That appointment involved some adjudication of complaints by citizens regarding the Canadian Security Intelligence Service (CSIS), and I did not want any appearance of conflict in that new role. But there was also steady disenchantment with both the federal and Ontario New Democratic parties, and in particular their failure to embrace fully the need for change and to practise balance in all aspects of policy, both domestic and foreign.

Since my resignation, I have had a chance to work on a number of fascinating challenges: the review of Canada's intelligence and security services, with SIRC; the restructuring of the Canadian Red Cross and the Toronto Symphony Orchestra; issues of federal governance around the world, with the Forum of Federations; the softwood lumber dispute; the fishing dispute at Burnt Church, New Brunswick; the review of higher education for the Dalton McGuinty government in Ontario; and the inquiry into the 1985 Air India terrorist bombing. Throughout it all, I worked as a lawyer on negotiation, mediation, and corporate governance, served on boards, raised money for charities, and helped to restructure many other organizations. It has hardly been a retirement!

The review of CSIS, which continued even more intensively with my Air India inquiry, brought home the challenge of reconciling the protection of security and the maintenance of civil liberties. The difficulty of this balance was, of course, heightened by 9/11 and even more recently by the arrests in June 2006 in Ontario based on allegations of a terrorist bomb plot.

In my experience with SIRC and through subsequent work in Sri Lanka and with the victims of the Air India tragedy, I have come to know the risks of living in a dangerous world.

Isolated as we may feel from the troubles of the Middle East, South Asia, or even central London, we are in the world, and the world is in us.

The Air India bombing was conceived, planned, and carried out in Canada. A bomb was built in British Columbia, placed on a plane in Toronto, and loaded aboard a flight bound for India. All 329 people aboard flight 182 were killed in an instant. The face of violence may be new, but there is nothing new about extremism.

The challenge of recognizing extremism and its potential for violence tests all of us, including our security and policing services. They were at the heart of the security and intelligence failures in 1985. To a significant extent, air safety was revamped in the immediate wake of Air India and has been again since 9/11, but the circumstances that surrounded the activities were more complex. It has been apparent from my undertakings with SIRC that the RCMP and CSIS have made notable progress in working together since then. This was evident through the joint appearance at their press conference announcing the arrest of the seventeen terrorist suspects in June 2006 in Toronto. Seamless co-operation and working within their mandates, but closely with each other when necessary, is critical to ensuring the transition from an intelligence investigation to a law enforcement operation in order to save lives and hold to account those who are violating our most basic laws.

· 4 ·

CSIS has come a long way since 1985, when it was an agency in its infancy, focused to a great extent on the Cold War. And it will have to keep changing, in an effort to respond to newer threats with different aims.

An even broader challenge to our society is to make sure we respond to the threat of violence fully within the best traditions of Canadian values. Those principles, along with our basic rights, are safeguarded by the Charter of Rights and Freedoms, which has been upheld by the courts. But they lie in public opinion as well.

Incidents of terror and threats to the safety of the public can test our sense of equality, tolerance, openness, and the compact with our fellow citizens that is the basis of the civil society we have enjoyed in this country. It has been suggested that some levels of coercive interrogation are acceptable: I disagree. Canada should not get carried away by the moment.

We must protect cherished values. We must do it as citizens. Governments alone cannot ensure the outcome. Public confidence in our system of justice and in the fundamental features of our free society must persevere. We must keep our perspective and hold sight of basic values when we react to such incidents. Our society must resist any backlash. The growth of intolerance or hate that can take root in the wake of alleged terror plots in the name of a religion or a cause poses the strongest challenge to citizens as well as to governments.

How Canada responds will be a profound test of our values and our capacities as a country.

My involvement in constitutional matters over many years led to the fascinating challenge of working on federal governance around the world. I became the founding chair of the Forum of Federations, an international non-governmental organization based in Ottawa that now has members ranging from Mexico to India. We sponsored a successful conference in Mont Tremblant, Quebec, attended by President Bill Clinton, Prime Minister Jean Chrétien, and many other heads of state in 1999, and began work around the world.

The Forum was, and is, all about governance, sharing experiences, building on Canada's own history of federalism, and creating a worldwide dialogue on diversity, conflict, and the need for governments to change.

My work with the Forum led to invitations to visit Sri Lanka, a country in turmoil. I have been back many times.

The island nation of nearly 20 million people has endured a harsh civil conflict for more than a generation. Simmering disputes about language, religion, jobs, and political power have grown into an intractable guerrilla war.

It seems a long way from the tropical beauty of Sri Lanka to Canada – but because we have the largest Tamil diaspora community, and have (so far successfully) coped with our deep cultural and linguistic divides, Sri Lankans have turned to Canada for support in their peace negotiations.

It is proving difficult. South Africa, the most outstanding example of peaceful constitutional change in recent times, achieved its success because remaking the constitution was ultimately seen as an issue that transcended partisan politics. This is decidedly not the case in Sri Lanka, where the subordination of peacemaking to interparty rivalry has made nation-building extraordinarily difficult.

There's also a question about the real willingness to share power. Violence against civilian populations, the assassination of political opponents, the recruitment of children into guerrilla units: such means are an affront to any notion of the rule of law and are incompatible with democracy and federalism. They are happening every day in Sri Lanka.

The challenge ahead is great indeed. It requires unambiguous commitment from the majority both to pluralism and the principle of self-determination within a single country. And it requires a commitment to the rule of law and non-violent change. Constitutional change must be transparent, and persuasive even to the farmers and spice-traders in the countryside. It cannot be done by stealth by urban elites.

The modern federal idea first and foremost implies a respect for people's identities and their political choices. The renewed interest in the federal idea is not confined to countries that have a federalist tradition. Ethnic, linguistic, racial, and religious conflicts have become the dominant issues facing the world order today. Wars after 1945 have been as much within countries as between them; it is no longer soldiers dying in the millions, but civilians.

From Rwanda to Cambodia, from the Balkans to East Timor, the battleground is within countries that are unable to resolve conflicts. In Sri Lanka, both Tamils and Sinhala bear the cultural scars of civil war: The Tamils' revered library at Jaffna, repository of their sacred texts, was destroyed, and the Sinhalese Buddhists' most holy site, the Temple of the Sacred Relic Tooth in the southern city of Kandy, was damaged. These are painful tragedies and are not easy things to "get past" or forget.

It is in this context that the federal idea is struggling to re-emerge. In Sri Lanka, negotiations need to focus on practical arrangements for both dividing and sharing power, for civil rights for minorities, for linguistic and religious tolerance. If Sri Lanka is to have a federal system, what precisely are the provinces (or states) to be and what are the boundaries? Are we dealing with a two-province solution, or a multi-province solution? What should be federal powers, and what provincial powers? Is Sri Lanka willing to consider asymmetrical federalism?

What guarantees would be in place for Sri Lanka's racial, linguistic, and religious minorities – not only as the indigenous Buddhist Sinahala and Hindu Tamils, but also as its small Muslim minority and hill-country Tamils who arrived in the nineteenth century to pick tea on British colonial plantations? Will they all be protected by an entrenched charter of rights enforceable by the courts? What steps will be taken to deal with the crimes of the past?

It is difficult to see how peace negotiations can progress unless such questions are dealt with. When Sri Lanka won independence more than half a century ago, it was one of the most fortunate countries in South Asia. Its people are educated and resourceful – but without peace, the vast potential of their island nation is squandered.

My Forum work also led me to an assignment in Iraq. I visited Iraqi Kurdistan in 2004 and Baghdad in 2005.

Deciding on the foundations of a country, and then writing them down, is a challenge at the best of times. The United States declared its independence in 1776 but only produced a new constitution eleven years later. The two largest provinces of nineteenth-century Canada quelled civil unrest in 1837, were told by the imperial power to merge three years later, and finally adopted a federal form of self-government together with the Maritime provinces in 1867. France has gone from republic to monarchy to republic again numerous times since 1789.

Iraq emerged as a country from the collapse of the Ottoman Empire at the end of the First World War. Its boundaries were the product of decisions by colonial masters. Saddam Hussein, who seized power through a military coup in the 1970s, used the arbitrary nature of these frontiers as his excuse for "liberating" the independent oil sheikdom of Kuwait in 1990. This prompted the first Gulf War. Ironically, one of the outcomes of the war was international protection of the Kurdish provinces in the north of the country, which has meant a relative degree of autonomy for that region since 1991.

The decision by the U.S./U.K.–led coalition to invade Iraq in the spring of 2003 had several consequences. The first was the ouster, and eventual capture, of Saddam Hussein. The second was the unleashing of several forces that the dictatorship had kept under firm control for generations, including a religious Shiite movement, largely in the south that seeks to see more traditional Islamic values enshrined and protected in the constitution. On the other hand, also emerging was the long-suppressed desire from other segments of the population for a liberal, secular democracy. This is comprised of a number of groups advocating women's rights, greater academic freedom, environmental protection, the protection of minorities, and the modernization of the Iraqi economy. The Kurds were strong supporters of the invasion, because it meant that the man responsible for their oppression would finally be brought to book. That overthrow could provide the basis for a protected constitutional status within a federal Iraq for the Kurdish people.

The decision, by the Americans, to disband the Iraqi army and police and to impose the strongest exclusion against members of the Ba'athist regime from participating in civic life had a devastating effect. It immediately created a vacuum in the maintenance of civil order, which left foreign armies to assume basic police responsibilities. Civil order in the centre of the country virtually collapsed. The decision also created a movement of the downwardly mobile and disaffected. Large portions of the public sector lost their jobs, their vocation, and their pensions. They were, for the most part, Sunni, and form an important base for the domestic insurgency that has engulfed Iraq since the premature declaration of victory by President George W. Bush several years ago.

To this maelstrom must be added even more ingredients: the terrorism of the bin Laden deputies, led
in Iraq by the late al-Zarqawi, who saw the vacuum of
civil order in Iraq as a promising breeding ground;
neighbouring countries, each with a different stake in
Iraq's continuing failure and weakness; and a tribalism
whose full force had been pushed down by Hussein's
army and bureaucracy but that now had very little to
hold it back.

My experiences in Iraq and Sri Lanka have led me to
draw certain conclusions about successful nation-building.

The first is that participants in nation-building have to
relinquish partisanship. Constitution-making, strengthening an existing federation, has to be seen as a pan-
political process. If we look at some classic examples
(America between 1776 and 1787, Canada from 1840 to
1867, South Africa in the remarkable period after Nelson
Mandela's release from prison), political rivals agreed, for
a time, to work together on a common project.

The second is that nation-building is most successful
when it is a post-conflict activity. Freedom and order are
sometimes treated as opposites. They are not. Order is
essential for the realization of freedom. Put colloquially,
shotgun marriages make for bad constitutions, for constitutions that will not last. Bringing violence to an end
is a precondition for successful change.

There has to be a pan-political agreement not only on
process, but also on fundamental values, on "ground
norms" for the constitution. These can be enormously
difficult to achieve in countries where there are religious
and ethnic divides. The key to success may be in agreeing

to leave things out of a constitution, and in accepting that not all private or community values can or should be constitutionally entrenched. That does not mean they are unimportant, but it does mean that everyone has to accept that the constitutional expression of them would simply be too divisive.

The most successful exercises are those that transcend not only party, but also ethnicity, race, religion, sectionalism, and geography. The will of the majority is not the only test, because viable states in divided societies also require the consent and participation of minorities. It cannot be achieved without leadership. The greatest example in our time is that of Nelson Mandela, who emerged from a quarter-century behind bars without bitterness. He embodies the qualities necessary for reconciliation. Calm, clear, generous, recognition of the point of view of the other, a deep sense of the dignity of each person, a steely-willed commitment to justice in the search for solutions. Unfortunately, there are not enough Mandelas in the world.

These processes are, above all, about legitimacy and respect for the rule of law. The difficulty in Iraq is that there is deep division about the legitimacy of the invasion and the means used to overthrow Saddam Hussein's regime. There is still the tremendous challenge of establishing order. Liberators can very quickly become occupiers.

The Canadian Constitution gives to the federal government the responsibility to ensure the "peace, order and good government" of the country, together with specific responsibilities, and indeed sovereignties, to both our federal and provincial governments. We have added the Charter of Rights and Freedoms as a foundation of our law. So, as a country we are committed to civic order and human rights.

As Canadians, we know only too well that a federal form of government means both self-rule and shared rule. We are familiar with the bickering and blaming that this often entails. But we should not take for granted the civility and respect for differences that we have achieved collectively throughout our history. We are also not alone: 40 per cent of the world's peoples live in federal countries.

If Canada is to play a useful role in this increasingly divided and dangerous world, we shall have to rely on our capacity for both peacemaking and peacekeeping. It will mean new roles for our military, including an ability to deal with the causes of conflict. It will mean a combination of diplomatic and humanitarian efforts as well.

In the years right after the Second World War, Canadians understood instinctively that the splendid isolationism that had marked so much of our thinking in earlier years had to give way to a stronger sense of engagement. The world's nations needed to commit to collective security and to regular multilateral engagement in order to create a more peaceable world. We endorsed the North Atlantic Treaty Organization (NATO) and the American Marshall Plan because we understood that a secure world required a real commitment. Putting Europeans back to work in growing countries was a critical element in ensuring the success of democracy. Canadians were at the table, important players in helping to create the United Nations, NATO, the Bretton Woods agreement. We invented the concept of peacekeeping out of the Suez Crisis. Canada lacks a colonialist past, having been a colony ourselves. Our history of peaceable immigration also adds to our reputation as a nation capable of tolerance, respect for others, and balanced solutions.

This is the spirit in which Canada commits, and why Canada is so well respected in the world today. To me, ours has been a wise and courageous approach.

Some of the most dangerous and difficult conflicts in the world will only be resolved where warring sides can accept the legitimacy of other people; where people who speak different languages and worship different gods can also accept the right of the neighbours to live as well; where those who are unable to accept these rights are firmly prevented by the rule of law and its enforcement from abusing others.

Throughout this time, I also acted as counsel to the Free Trade Lumber Council, a national industry association of lumber producers committed to free and fair access to international markets for Canadian companies.

Millions of Canadians owe their jobs and their standard of living to our ability to take care of our great forests, to harvest them, to add value to them in a variety of ways, and to sell what we produce. Ensuring sustainable forest practices is essential to the long-term viability of this industry. Canadians have been exporting lumber from the time of early settlement, to Europe, to the United States, and now throughout the world. Without these exports, Canada would lose hundreds of thousands of jobs. Because of intense market competition, particularly from Scandinavia and the Baltic countries, the Canadian industry has invested a great deal in research and development of new value-added products and continues to ask the perennial question of how to get more value from each tree cut. It is this pattern of enhanced investment that makes the Canadian industry competitive in world markets.

Since the recession of the late 1970s, lumber has been the subject of intense debate, of trade actions, of temporary agreements, of ad hoc ways of sidelining the constant pressure from the demands for protection coming from many American producers. The political and other pressures brought to bear meant that lumber became the Great Exception throughout the negotiations over the U.S.–Canada Free Trade Agreement and the North American Free Trade Agreement (NAFTA).

Those trade agreements were the subject of intense debate in Canada, as they were in the United States. Their argument was that rules-based, open, and transparent trade is in the end better than the alternatives, and that as a country whose economy is more than 50 per cent based on trade, it only made sense, together with our adherence to the World Trade Organization (WTO), for Canada to find a clear basis in rules and international law for our access to markets outside Canada.

The premise of these agreements is that it is not really open to any of us to retreat into protectionism. Once that starts to happen, others will do the same. Open trade is always a two-way street.

The battles over lumber even have their own Roman numerals. We speak of Lumber I, II, III, and IV, and many are rubbing their hands in eager anticipation of Lumber V. From a Canadian perspective, these are battles we have to fight in the halls and corridors of American trade law, and on appeal and review we always seem to win, yet we find that the political pressures are such, and the imbalance in our relationship so great, that some kind of restraints always end up being imposed: and so we go once again from countervailing duty to the memorandum of understanding, from export tax to quota restrictions.

This is hardly the world of free trade and open markets. It is a reversion to the old world of protection and imposed agreements.

We hear the tired lines that the provinces subsidize the industry, that log export restraints are unfair, that the federal government and the provinces don't have environmental laws as strong as the Americans, and that this amounts to a subsidy as well. We are told that Canadian railways subsidize logs, and that the Canadian dollar itself is a problem.

The only problem with these arguments is that they are not true. They are demonstrably false, and no amount of political pressure will make them true.

The subsidy argument is wrong, from beginning to end. No objective analysis has succumbed to its wiles. It will not withstand the light of day, or the power of reason. It is sustained by old-fashioned self-interest and the shopworn rhetoric of U.S. protectionism.

What to make of Prime Minister Stephen Harper's recent deal with President George W. Bush on softwood?

Harper has described it as "win-win." But is it? Under the deal, the Canadian industry gets back less than 80 per cent of the billions left on deposit. Canadian exports will be subject to a quota and an export tax if lumber prices fall below $350 per thousand board feet. The Americans have conceded nothing, and continue to maintain the falsehood that the Canadian industry is unfairly subsidized.

What really happened is that an industry under siege is being pressured to agree to a deal because the Canadian government told them nothing more could be done, and this was the best that could be achieved. But a fundamental objective of both the Free Trade Agreement and NAFTA, a respected dispute settlement mechanism, has now been cast aside by Stephen Harper.

In the late summer of 2000, the minister of fisheries and oceans asked me to go to Burnt Church, New Brunswick, to mediate a difficult dispute over lobster fishing. A Supreme Court decision in the Donald Marshall Jr. case had recognized Aboriginal fishing rights flowing from the treaties of the eighteenth century. The Burnt Church reserve immediately became the nucleus of a highly charged confrontation.

My involvement in the dispute focused on an immediate effort to lower tension and to avoid violence. The longer term solution – a reworking of licences, assistance to the band for boats, and an acceptance by everyone of the importance of conservation – took a longer time. Eight days of non-stop discussions and negotiation were intense and emotional but a profound reminder that the encounter between the first Canadians and settlers is ongoing, and there are still many key issues to resolve.

To my work on softwood and Burnt Church was soon added a new challenge: a review of Ontario's post-secondary education system.

Premier Dalton McGuinty gave me a chance to immerse myself in a subject that had long been a passion: education. While polls show that the public is more concerned about health care than other areas of policy, we won't have a health-care system worthy of the name if we do not earn the money that allows us to fund it.

We cannot have a social justice agenda or a social welfare agenda if we do not also have a prosperity agenda, and we need to understand the connection between the two. They are not separate. They are very much inter-twined in the making of public policy.

We have tended as Canadians to invest too little in the future. That pattern needs to change. Education is the one policy that combines prosperity and opportunity. In our own lives, the chance for an education is the moment of opportunity that for most of us determines the difference between poverty and prosperity.

I was brought up on two stories: the first was my grandmother's deep disappointment that she was not allowed to go to school past the age of twelve because at that time in Scotland most girls were expected to leave school and go out to work. The second is what she took from that experience. Nell Rae implanted in my father the firm conviction that he had to go to university. A $200 bursary in 1932 allowed him to do that. Those stories are replicated thousands and thousands of times in our country.

If you take a grade nine class today, a full quarter of that class will not finish grade twelve. In some parts of the province, it's much higher than that; in Aboriginal high schools, it can be as high as 70 per cent. Another quarter that complete high school will not go on to post-secondary education. Well over half the jobs that are being created today require some form of post-secondary education. Herein lies the challenge.

When I was in university in the late 1960s and 1970s, less that one in ten students went to university and we didn't have a community college system. So we've come a long way. But we still have to move ahead.

In my "Leader in Learning" report submitted in February 2005, I documented the fact that we are on the edge of a major demographic change for which we are unprepared. Skills shortages across business and industry, a distinct mismatch between the abilities of immigrants and their real opportunities in Canada, high debt levels for some, but not all, students, growing class sizes, and clear deterioration in the quality of the student experience: these are undeniable facts.

So, too, was the evidence of under-investment in education compared to other fields. In a shrinking world, we quite rightly pay attention to how others are doing, how we measure up. My message was, and is, blunt. Canada is falling behind, and given the undeniable link between prosperity and investment in higher education, this is extremely short-sighted. A downward spiral has to be stopped.

My report concluded that every society has relied for its survival on the transfer of skills and abilities from generation to generation. What is new is the level and breadth of knowledge and skill required to make our way in the world. The wealth of our citizens now depends much more on the power of our brains. Today our standards of living, and consequently our quality of life, depend on people having access to education that is on par with the best in the world. Not everyone will have a post-secondary education, but most people should. When half of our children are missing the experience, we are losing potential.

Industrial societies all over the world are considering how to improve higher education. China and India are investing unprecedented amounts in their post-secondary institutions and research. The United Kingdom has just completed a major public policy debate on the issue and has recently announced three-year commitments for funding to universities and research councils. The world is not standing still. Neither should Canada.

Some will argue that quality and high standards are incompatible with the desire to make education more accessible. Others may contend that the central goal of social inclusiveness should trump "elitist" concerns about excellence, that Canada can afford a pretty good system but not one that can achieve greatness.

Each of these views is wrong. We need governments and institutions that are irrevocably committed to access for every Canadian who is qualified to attend. Because the new economy demands it, the number of people attending will rise substantially in the years ahead. We also need governments and institutions that are unwaveringly committed to excellence in teaching and research. Opportunity and excellence are both diminished when we invest less than we should, or when institutions are reluctant to focus and insist on better outcomes.

The government of Ontario responded favourably to many of my recommendations, particularly the need for more funding on a multi-year basis. I argued in my report that steady, multi-year increases were necessary to bring Ontario up to the Canadian average, but that even more dramatic increases were going to be required to allow us to compete effectively at the international level.

The federal government's investments in research and innovation in the late 1990s helped prevent a dangerous slide to mediocrity. Its efforts now should focus on four areas:

1. a renewed and substantial investment in graduate education
2 a renewal of their focus on skills and training
3. a major expansion of international experience for students, and
4. a clearer direction on ensuring access and affordability for students.

When I began my report in 2004, I discovered a profound sense of pessimism in the institutions – the feeling was that no one in government really seemed concerned about the state of higher education. The student movement was, and is, divided, with some more concerned about the deteriorating quality of education and some fixated on the issue of cost to the student.

Governments should be doing everything they can to ensure that student aid – federal, provincial, and institution-based – is genuinely progressive. We must never lose sight that it is living costs, foregoing income, the fear of assuming debt, as well as tuition that are the real economic factors in student choice.

In short, governments have to learn to let colleges and universities be their best, and to provide a living income to students to let them get on with their studies. There needs to be a new federal-provincial agreement on higher education.

In my report, I wrote:

I am urging the provincial government to adopt as a key mission for the province the goal for Ontario to be a leader in learning, and to fund higher education accordingly, with measured increases over the next several years. The commitment that every qualified student in Ontario should find a place in college or university regardless of means should be enshrined in new legislation. I am recommending that the walls between colleges and universities continue to come down, that administrations accept the need for more transparency, accountability and collaboration. I am urging the federal government to recognize that it must become a reliable and steady partner in that mission, and in particular should become an ally in the expansion of skilled trades and graduate studies. I am asking students to recognize that they are significant beneficiaries of education and that tuition levels that fairly reflect the value of that education are reasonable, provided the governments do their job and provided there are real improvements in quality and student assistance. I am also urging a major reform of student assistance, with the principle that lower-income students should receive direct grants from the government, that all students should have access to loans that reflect the actual cost of study and cost of living, and that both levels of government should make loan repayment more flexible in timing and more sensitive to the incomes that graduates are in fact earning.

Leadership will bring change. The change has to be sustainable. There are enough public and private resources in this province to build first-class institutions of higher education, to make them both accessible and affordable to an ever-widening cross-section of the public and to provide education to our students that is truly excellent. I hope this review contributes to achieving these goals.

Just as my work on higher education was coming to an end, Anne McLellan, the federal minister of public safety, asked me to review the investigation of the Air India bombing. Two individuals who had been charged with

organizing the conspiracy to kill 329 people on board the
Air India flight from Toronto to London on June 23,
1985, were acquitted after a lengthy trial. There was naturally a deep-seated sense of frustration on the part of the
Air India families and, indeed, all Canadians.

I described what happened in the opening passage of
my report, "Lessons to Be Learned":

In the early morning hours of June 23rd, 1985, Air
India Flight 182 approached the west coast of Ireland.
The flight began in Toronto, receiving passengers and
luggage from connecting flights, and picking up more
in Mirabel, Quebec. Children of all ages were joined
by their families, looking forward to visiting their
loved ones and friends in India. Most of the passengers were Canadians. Given the time of year – late
June marks the beginning of summer holidays here in
Canada – there were an especially large number of
young adults, children and entire families traveling on
the flight.

Unbeknownst to them, in the weeks prior to that
flight, a group of Canadians had been planning to blow
up the plane. The conspiracy was based in radical
sections of the Sikh community in Vancouver and elsewhere who were pursuing the goal of an independent
country, to be called Khalistan, in the northwestern
province of Punjab in India.

As a result of this conspiracy, a bomb was manu-
factured, placed in a suitcase, and taken to the
Vancouver airport, where on June 22, 1985, it was
checked through on a flight from Vancouver to

Toronto. In Toronto, the lethal suitcase made its way onboard Air India Flight 181, which then stopped at Mirabel and became Air India Flight 182, en route to London and Delhi.

At approximately 12:14 a.m., on June 23, 1985, the timer on the bomb detonated a charge and blew open a hole in the left aft fuselage of the plane. The aircraft, which bore the name 'Kanishka', was blown apart, falling approximately 31,000 feet below into the Atlantic Ocean off the south-west coast of Ireland.

The children going to visit grandparents, young tourists looking forward to their first experience of India, women and men of all ages, flight attendants and pilots, in short all 329 passengers and crew were killed.

It was, at that point, and up until 9/11, the worst act of terrorism against the traveling public in world history.

It was an intense assignment. There was deep resentment on the part of the families at what they perceived was a failed surveillance of terrorist activity and a failed investigation of the bombing. My work led me to conclude that for many years Canadian governments had not responded adequately to the bombing, either in recognizing the extent of the loss suffered or in realizing the breakdown of communication that made preventing and prosecuting these crimes more difficult.

The experience affected me greatly. It is impossible to talk with the families without being profoundly affected by their dignity and determination to find answers. It also

reminded me that terrorism is not an abstraction foreign
to the Canadian experience.

In my report, I urged the government to carry on with
a thorough review and inquiry to make sure a similar
event would not happen, and to ensure that the responsible government agencies had fixed the problems in their
relationship. The Paul Martin government asked me to
keep going in my work.

After the election of January 23, 2006, the Stephen
Harper government decided that it would prefer a full-
fledged judicial inquiry to the more focused policy task I
had called for in my report.

The Harper election also led to a decision by Paul
Martin to leave the leadership of the Liberal Party. A few
months later, I announced my decision to join the race to
succeed him.

I have spent the past thirty years deeply involved in
politics and public service. From federal politics to
the premier's office in Ontario, I have worked on some
of the most complex problems that Canada – and the
world – face.

I decided to enter the leadership race because I believe
politics and public service matter. That has been the moti-
vating force throughout my working life. I am running
because I care deeply about my country. I want it to stay
strong. I want it to stay together. And I want to play
whatever part I can to help make those things happen.

I have learned from hard experience the costs of the
ideology that Stephen Harper and the Conservatives

want to impose on Canada, and that Canadians in a majority voted against in the last election. I am running as a Liberal for the leadership of the Liberal Party because I have learned that Canada needs a party that is committed to change, that is open to all Canadians, and that understands that politics is about people, not theories and ideologies.

Sir Wilfrid Laurier talked of his "sunny ways," and reminded Canadians that faith and love are more important than doubt and hate. I like the Liberal Party because it is optimistic, because it builds on hope, not fear, because it believes in opportunity for everyone, because it is inclusive. My dad always used to say about certain people, "He's a big person, he's a builder." For me, the glass is always half full. I love this country and all its people, and for me the Liberal Party best expresses those feelings.

There are some basic lessons I've drawn from my experiences as an active politician, premier, and mediator and problem-solver over the last thirty years. In part, this is the story of how I have come to embrace the Liberal way.

The first lesson I learned is what I call the Ella Fitzgerald lesson: "I've been rich and I've been poor, and rich is better." Prosperity and the encouragement of prosperity are critical. Not simply desirable, they are vital to improving the lot of our citizens today and those who will join us here in the future. I governed during the worst recession since the 1930s. The prosperity of the late 1980s came to a dramatic halt. Immediately, we learned of the difficulties that that entailed. Many business people have told me that in good times mistakes can be quickly overcome. In tough times, that is just not the case.

Since my time as premier of Ontario, Canada has developed a collective allergy to deficits, and that is a good thing. In some ways that has become as much a part of our political identity as quality health care. We must continue to keep our fiscal house in order.

We need competitive tax and regulatory policies, but they must be balanced by a renewed focus on learning, on innovation, and investments in infrastructure that encourage private and public investment. This was a key focus of the Chrétien-Martin years. They are not, apparently, on the Harper priority list. Harper's idea of economic policy is to take a point off the GST. His right hand doesn't know what his far right hand is doing. It just isn't enough for a complex economy like Canada's.

It's a tough, competitive world out there. Preparing Canadians for the challenge ahead is at the top of my list. It needs to be a focus of our politics again. But as important as prosperity is, it is not enough. It must be matched with purpose.

Wealth creation must be a partner to shared opportunity. Children living in poverty are a challenge to our conscience and to our future. Child poverty challenges our sense of what *makes* sense – we know full well that generations left behind will be more likely to fall ill, to go to jail, to need constant support. Canadians deserve better.

I've learned that trying to turn heads is more important than counting heads. Taking what my father called the pulse of democracy should not deter people from understanding that things change – and that things *must* change. Henry Ford said, "If I'd asked people what they wanted, I'd have given them a faster horse." We need to listen – but we also need to lead.

Ending child poverty is where we can lead. It can be, should be, a goal of our government. First reducing it, then eliminating it.

To do that you have to begin at the beginning. With health care, with early learning and child development, with high-quality and affordable child care, with the social safety net that defines us as Canadians.

We need a health-care strategy that ensures our public system is accessible, safe, of high quality, and includes a focus on wellness and prevention, especially in the early years. The federal government must come to the health-care table as a player and a partner to help ensure these ends.

When a quarter of our high-school students drop out, and a further 25 per cent graduate school without going on, we have a problem. When students' perception of the costs of higher education is greater than their sense of the value that comes from post-secondary skills, we have a problem. As Canadians, we have to strive for better.

During the last federal election campaign I was struck, like many Canadians, by the absence of discussion from the major political parties of Canada's place in the world. It is no secret, no astounding revelation, that our well-being depends on what is happening around us. Our economic health is dependent on our trade with partners across the globe as well as just across the border. Our citizens come from every region of the world.

As Canadians, we would do well to remember the respect we have gained internationally – our reputation for stability and fairness and as a country that works. But that is not enough. It must be matched by a commitment to meet our international obligations, and then do more to lead.

A foreign policy borne of an ideology and excessive rhetoric is bound to fail – we have heard the reverberations of such failure echo 'round the world. Jean Chrétien was right about Canada and Iraq – not because he was following public opinion, but because he thought the invasion ill-advised and contrary to international law. It was a judgment call that was fundamentally sound, reflected our values, and offered our independent voice.

Like all the major problems that face our world, Canada cannot solve the environmental degradation and global warming alone. But we should be more of a leader. Signing the Kyoto Protocol was only the first step – accepting targets is one thing, achieving them is another. It would be nice to say that retreat from Kyoto is unthinkable. But, in fact, we know with the current government it is not. Mr. Harper has put us on notice: the Kyoto Protocol is of no importance to him. I disagree. Our environment – our children's future – is not negotiable.

The Conservatives are attempting to take us down paths that do not reflect our strengths or speak to our most pressing challenges. On foreign policy, Canada's voice has gone missing under the Conservatives. Most Canadians support Kyoto, child care, and rights for minorities. They want to see us investing in education, health care, and research and innovation. Canadians want and deserve an alternative that is hopeful, generous, dedicated to building prosperity and sharing opportunity. I want to help shape that alternative and get our country back on track.

The sooner, the better.

I have learned a great deal about federalism. I worked on and supported the Meech and Charlottetown Accords, but in recent years the experience of working with nations struggling to create their own federalism has also deepened my appreciation for what we have achieved in Canada. The Liberal Party of Canada has a fine tradition in building federalism that needs to be remembered and revered. From Laurier to Martin, Liberals have understood the twin need to be sensitive to the concerns of Quebec and French Canadians without compromising the ability to relate directly to all the citizens of Canada. Reconciliation and a deepened relationship with Aboriginal peoples is a further challenge to which our federal system can and must respond. Throughout my career, I have been a passionate advocate of federalism. Canada needs common institutions to advance our common purpose. Political relations can always be improved, and ultimately we share far more than divides us.

I have had extraordinary opportunities to serve over the years. Every project has introduced me to more Canadians, taught me more about what is meaningful to us, shown me more about who we are as a people.

From Burnt Church to softwood lumber, from terrorism to education, I have been forced to think of practical, workable solutions to seemingly intractable problems. I cannot claim to have always succeeded. I bear, as Teddy Roosevelt once said, the scars of having fought in the arena. But the arena is where one learns how to fight for what one believes in – and how to win.

—=◆=—

CHAPTER TWO

Why Politics Matters

POLITICS IS IN BAD REPUTE. POLITICIANS RANK AT the very bottom of the "most trusted" list. Fewer Canadians vote. Among Canadians under the age of twenty-five, it is estimated that as many as 75 per cent didn't turn up at the polls in the 2000 election. In 2006, nearly 15 million Canadians voted. More than 8 million chose not to participate.

There is often a tendency to imagine an idyllic past when political life was seen as a distinguished calling. This is a bit of an exaggeration.

Sir John A. Macdonald's government was pilloried for giving a special benefit to a group of investors in the

Canadian Pacific Railway. He sent a famous telegram asking for another $10,000 for his election campaign. Macdonald's government was defeated, but he returned to office in 1876 and served as prime minister until his death in 1891.

When Sir Wilfrid Laurier declined to join Robert Borden's War Cabinet, the election of 1917 was marked by riots and demonstrations, and he was dubbed "the Kaiser's candidate."

The men generally regarded as the giants of twentieth-century politics, Franklin Roosevelt and Winston Churchill, went through their political lives often as vilified as they were admired. Heading to a convention victory in 1932, Roosevelt had the endorsement of not a single newspaper. Churchill, the lion of the western world, was defeated in the general election of 1945.

So the idea that there was once a time when leaders were universally admired, trusted, and loved is untrue. But still, there is something uniquely difficult about the times in which we are living. We are living in a low-trust world.

People often resort to saying, "We'd be better off without politics." Yet politics is an inescapable fact of life. Robinson Crusoe no doubt did without it, but as soon as Friday came along politics arrived as well. U.S. political scientist Harold Lasswell defined politics as "who gets what, when, where, and how." Crusoe was in a position of power and authority. Decisions were made. Work was done.

Modern ideas of freedom, equality, and democracy came along as traditional justifications for power and authority became less compelling and acceptable. But let's not forget how long and slow this progress has been. There was a property qualification for voting until the twentieth century. Women were only allowed to vote in 1917, and not until 1940 in Quebec. Chinese immigrants to Canada had to pay a head tax and couldn't vote until 1947. Members of Canada's Aboriginal communities were eligible to enlist in the First and Second World Wars, but could not vote until 1960.

When the first European settlers came to Canada, they came face to face with traditional Aboriginal societies that governed themselves by consensus, that relied on the land for their living, and that passed on values through generations of ritual and tradition.

The clash of values and communities that followed was dramatic and painful. The settlers brought with them illnesses like smallpox to which the first Canadians had no resistance. They died in the hundreds of thousands. The impact of military conquest and disease wiped out the Beothuk people of Newfoundland entirely.

We are today the living inheritors of this conflict and its outcome. We cannot escape the politics of what happened.

The liberal democratic idea in Canadian politics began when the settlers of the early nineteenth century insisted that the governing authorities around them respond to their needs. Whether the Family Compacts of Toronto, Montreal, or Halifax, the Tory elite of those years reflected little of the interests or values of the majority. Closed, secretive, authoritarian, and smug, the inner

circle insisted they were closer to God. They were certainly closer to power. It took a rebellion and dramatic
reform to replace the tight little compacts with responsible government.

With this new expansion of the democratic franchise
came dramatic improvements such as public schools
and universities, municipal reform and leadership for a
burgeoning economy. In 1867, Canada as a modern federation was born.

Since then, each generation of Canadians has learned
that politics matters, that people working together for a
common cause can make a difference. Those Canadians
who know first-hand the totalitarian experience often say
they have come to Canada to "get away from politics."
The twentieth century has been bedevilled by the lure of
ideologies that promise a heaven on earth, that impose
tyrannies in the name of this bogus secular salvation.

The foundation of both the liberal democratic and
federal idea is that there are limits to politics – indeed,
limits to government itself. The decision to introduce a
Charter of Rights and Freedoms is really a reflection of
that principle: the rule of law applies not only to citizens,
but also to governments. Since that time, the Supreme
Court of Canada has made it clear that the Charter is
intended to require all Canadian governments to respect
the rights that citizens have by virtue of their very
humanity and their membership in Canadian society.

If the issue of the balance between citizens' rights and
governments is now firmly at the centre of the work of
our legislatures and courts – whether the issue is the

right of same-sex couples to share access to marriage and partnership, the right of patients to timely treatment for critical operations, or the right of women to equal pay for work of equal value – liberal democratic politics has also been about the relative roles of market and government, the private sector and the public sector.

The explorations of Jacques Cartier and Samuel de Champlain were sponsored by governments. The loyalists who left the United States to come to what became the provinces of Canada after the American Revolution were political refugees. The immigrants who built the Rideau Canal – the biggest infrastructure project in the British Empire at the time – were given Crown land by the government.

The merchants and fur trappers who worked for the rival North West Company and then the Hudson's Bay Company were adventurers working with government monopolies and licences.

Public ownership and private enterprise encouraged and sanctioned by government is clearly an integral part of the Canadian experience. Macdonald's National Policy protected manufacturers – largely in central Canada – and forced Canadian farmers and consumers to pay more to support them. The working people who made industrialization happen joined unions and insisted on a better provision of social insurance, whether workers' compensation or support for the unemployed.

The dream of a society where everyone works together without property or rights is, as we have discovered, a nightmare. The security of the person and property – with limits to government, and where other rights are respected – is a necessary basis for a decent society. We know that economies that are run by states are dramatically less successful than those that are responsive to the marketplace.

· 37 ·

This is now a settled question for much of the world. Its irrevocable symbol is the collapse of the Berlin Wall in 1989, the wall built to keep Germans from leaving the east for the west. As President John F. Kennedy so rightly pointed out, no one was ever shot going the other way. The current political debate is about a less catastrophic range of choices than those that raged across Europe, Asia, and Africa in the twentieth century. Some observers have called this the "end of ideology," as if this is something to be lamented. It is not. But critical choices remain.

How do we make our economy more innovative, how do we ensure its productivity? How do we make sure it is sustainable? The expansion of the Industrial Revolution on a hitherto unimagined scale now means that the Earth's atmosphere is changing rapidly, with a directly consequential warming of the planet. Canada is a small nation compared to the giants around us, but we are as affected as any by the change in the global environment. The melting of the Arctic ice cap and the shifting of permafrost farther north affects people, communities, and all animal and plant life.

By "sustainability," we mean an environmental focus that has to build right into the value we attach to economic growth itself. It can't be an add-on or an afterthought.

But an environmental policy that is disconnected from the world of work, taxes, prices, and profits is also bound to be unsuccessful. Scientists tell us that environmental change can be reversed, but that it will take both immediate and concerted action. There is a temptation to blame "government" and "polluters" for the problem. But we as citizens elect and defeat governments. And our own behaviour as consumers, as well as that of billions of others, will have a lot to do with turning the weather around.

Politics, then, is at once personal, local, national, and global. We cannot escape it any more than we can escape the air we breathe. In fact, politics has a lot to say about the kind of air we breathe.

Rabbi Hillel, one of the great teachers in the Rabbinic tradition, who lived more than two thousand years ago, is said to have asked three questions that have become aphorisms for our time: "If I am not for myself, who will be for me? If I am only for myself, what am I? If not now, when?"

All good politics start with people. Tip O'Neill is famous for the expression "all politics is local." The local is about a place. It's also about identity. It is about self-interest, which is natural. At its worst, it can be narrow, exclusive, "all about me and my little platoon."

A politics that tells people only what they want to hear, that panders always and only to the question What are you going to do for me?, may work but not for long.

When I discuss politics with my children today, it is less about political parties and more about the environment, Canada's moral obligation to those living in poverty, making sure that opportunities in life are truly shared.

I don't think of them or their friends as disengaged, cynical, or "apolitical." They are not enamoured of polit-
ical parties as much as previous generations, they hate corruption, and they want and expect people in public life to practise what they preach (and to preach a little less). They know that politics is the art of the possible, that "the possible" is not fixed in stone but grows as people are moved by their idealism. They do not want to settle for third best.

On the environment, for example, they know that while what Canada does alone will not stop climate change, we shall have no credibility with others if we are a laggard and not a leader. That's why the idea of Canada dropping out of Kyoto, or not taking its obligations seriously, strikes them as so absurdly wrong-headed. And they're right.

Partisan affiliation is changing. Fewer people are wedded to one party or another – their attitude will change from election to election, from issue to issue, and from leader to leader. In the mid-nineteenth century, before radio, television, and now the Internet, views were more fixed and change was slower. Thousands would attend political rallies; a local speaker coming to town was an event, a source of inspiration, education, and entertainment.

The Internet and the twenty-four-hour news cycle have added to a culture of "info-tainment." The five-hundred-channel universe puts everyone on notice: market share is quickly gained and instantly lost. The

British prime minister Harold Wilson is famous for the expression "a week is a long time in politics." That could now be revised to "a sentence is a long time in politics."

A media culture where the task of journalism was once described as "to walk through a battlefield after the battle and shoot the survivors" adds fuel to the mix. I am not blaming journalists for the culture – only describing the world in which both the media and politicians live.

It is a world in which the universal temptation is to manipulate and control the impression made. It's called spin. It's hardly new. Sir John A. Macdonald was marketed mercilessly by his handlers. Sir Wilfrid Laurier's contemporaries complained of his extraordinary capacity to "bamboozle." But behind them both was substance as well as style. When politics becomes all froth and sizzle, something is very wrong. The public becomes cynical, and rightfully so.

Can the public's faith in the process be restored? Candour about spin and its excesses would be a good start. Laws on fundraising and accountability on how political parties conduct public business are part of the answer as well.

The recent publicity on how advertising agencies and political organizers took advantage of the Canadian government's program to sponsor events in Quebec (and across the country) has become a cause for further erosion of public confidence in institutions and parties. Not for the first time, corruption was a major issue in the last election.

All governments advertise. Making people aware of programs and sharing information is a good thing, not a bad thing. All governments and government agencies sponsor public events. Just about every county fair, fishing derby, and cultural festival in this country – from the Stratford Festival to la Fête de Chicoutimi – is looking for sponsorship from governments at every level.

Separatist rhetoric conveniently overlooks the reality that governments in Quebec engage heavily in advertising and sponsorship. We have to understand the exaggeration of the separatist spin: what they are telling the people of Quebec is that both the Liberal Party and the cause of federalism and Canada itself are corrupt because of the sponsorship program. The Conservatives and the NDP spent the last election making a slightly more modest claim, but made it with great fanfare, and to considerable effect: the Liberal Party, they said, is rotten to the core. Throw the bums out and all will be well.

Charles Krauthammer, the Canadian-born Conservative columnist, once observed that if Ford and General Motors engaged in nothing but negative spin about the safety and performance of their competitors' products, no one should be surprised if people stopped buying cars. It is the negativity of the political parties themselves that fuels public cynicism.

Those whose political objective is the independence of Quebec and the breakup of the Canadian federation will, of course, use every event and incident to fuel their argument. But that does not mean they should be allowed to get away with it. It was not wrong, let alone corrupt, for the Canadian government to sponsor public events in Quebec, or anywhere else. It was very wrong for companies and individuals to take advantage of the program, and to line their own pockets. They should be held to account.

Candour in the face of intense scrutiny by the media is a prerequisite. The world of the Internet and the blogger – where everyone can be a columnist and can have an opinion broadcast to the world – magnifies the scrutiny a thousand-fold. Is trust and confidence possible in such a world?

The answer is that it's more difficult. Conspiracy theories abound. Rumours are quickly spread. The pace of the spin cycle continues to quicken.

Yet it is important to remember that despite the spinning, buzzing, and cynicism, good government still matters. The mobilization of opinion that is required to reduce greenhouse emissions and to slow climate change, to give education a higher priority, to end child poverty – just to name three key priorities for Canada – requires leadership, the ability to inspire Canadians to some common goals and to put the practical steps in place to help get us there.

I spent twenty years of my life as a member of the New Democratic Party, and was elected eight times to federal and provincial Parliament as an NDP member. Why did I leave the NDP to join the Liberals?

I have described in my two earlier books, *From Protest to Power* and *The Three Questions*, the ups and downs of my political life before 1996 and the conclusions I reached as a result.

Simply put, after lengthy personal experience, I concluded that the federal NDP and its Ontario counterpart are wedded to a culture of opposition and protest. They

have great difficulty embracing the lessons of the postwar
world about the relationship between markets, society,
and government. Determined to be in Canada what one
of their leaders described as the "last, best, left," the New
Democrats are confining themselves to an ever-smaller
universe. They are ignoring obvious lessons of history,
solid research, and the example of other left-leaning
parties elsewhere, such as "new Labour" in Britain.

I resigned from the NDP when I became a member
of the Security Intelligence Review Committee in 1998.
I felt that job required scrupulous political neutrality, a
position I maintained throughout my time on SIRC. The
publication of *The Three Questions* in October 1998
marked the break in another way.

The argument I expressed in that book was that the
pursuit of wealth creation was not opposed to social
justice, as much thinking on the left seemed to imply.
Rather, good public policy required a commitment to a
balance between the self-interest of the market and the
broader claims of the public good.

Citing Edmund Burke's aphorism that "there is
nothing more dangerous than governing in the name of
a theory," the underlying theme of the book was the need
to avoid ideological enthusiasm. It seemed to me then, as
it does now, that both the right and the left have been
unable to avoid the lure of ideology.

At its core, the NDP, both in Ontario and federally,
has been more committed to protest than to seeing
the country achieve a balanced, progressive, effective
government. It cannot escape a knee-jerk reaction to
business entrepreneurship and wealth creation. Most

social democratic parties in power have had to address issues of marginal tax rates for businesses and individuals from an intensely practical viewpoint. Governments from Manitoba to Sweden have accepted that this is a precondition for prosperity. But the federal NDP's recent opposition to any tax changes for large and even small business is a sure sign that "private sector is bad, public sector is good" is a flawed mantra it simply can't avoid.

In the last federal election, the NDP's final pitch to any Liberal was to "please lend us your vote" for one election. The party of Pearson and Trudeau, the argument went, wasn't being represented by the current leadership: time in the penalty box would do the trick.

With a refreshed and refocused leadership, the Liberal Party is surely entitled to say to those same voters: "We are the party of Laurier, Pearson, and Trudeau. We are the party of prosperity, fairness, and pluralism. The NDP has not earned the right to retain your vote. We would like your vote back."

The roots of the Liberal Party of Canada lie in the power of two ideas: First, responsible government required the end of an unaccountable Family Compact and its replacement by reform-minded governments committed to expanding democracy and the public good.

Second, since, in Laurier's words, "Canada is a very difficult country to govern," the greatest care has to be paid to the sensitivities of French and English, the balance between regions, the never-ending issue of national unity, and the need to put our relationship with Aboriginal peoples on a new footing.

The Liberal Party's strength is its capacity for governing and statecraft, its determination to seek balance, and its underlying commitment to prosperity and the sharing of opportunity.

Jean Chrétien's election in 1993 and the crushing defeat of the Progressive Conservatives provided the party with a fresh chance to prove its strength and relevance to Canada's needs. The greatest achievement of those years was undoubtedly the elimination of the deficit and the return of real fiscal strength to the country.

To these must be added the decision to sign the Kyoto Protocol to the United Nations Framework Convention on Climate Change (Kyoto Protocol), the commitment to higher education, innovation and research, and Canada's renewed focus on international development and peace-making. Changes to Canada's election financing laws will also be seen as a critical legacy.

Paul Martin's accession to office in 2003 was quickly followed by an election in the spring of 2004. While only given a minority mandate, there were marked achievements of the Martin years, most notably the negotiation of the agreement known as the Kelowna Accord, a budget described by Greenpeace as "the greenest in Canadian history," and an historic agreement on child care negotiated by Liberal MP Ken Dryden that marked both federal leadership and provincial flexibility.

What kind of political party do we need to lead Canada into the future? A party that is proud of its history but not afraid of change. A party that embraces Canada in all its diversity and a world with all of its challenges. A party that seeks to govern on behalf of Canada's people but accepts its role in opposition when that is the public will.

The Liberal Party of Canada is that party. The next election will not be about protest or punishment. It will be about policies and people, ideas and leadership, and finding our voice again on the international stage.

CHAPTER THREE

The Cart and the Horse: Creating and Sharing a Sustainable Prosperity

WHENEVER WE DISCUSS CANADA'S FUTURE, PEOPLE come at it from a full range of perspectives.

In the world of politics and policy-making, it is only too easy to see things through a limited lens. So it is that the business person focuses on taxes, interest rates, government regulation, and the dollar; the environmentalist on pollution; the social worker on child poverty; and on it goes. Government departments tend to work and think in silos, advancing prescriptions that relate to the particular world in which they live and work.

One of government's great challenges is to break down the silos and the hardening of the categories that make good policy-making difficult. Canada needs to be competitive and prosperous. Canada needs to be fair and just. Canada needs to be sustainable and innovative.

These things go together. They are not separate. The banker needs to care about child poverty. The social activist needs to worry about productivity. They both need to insist that Canada be a leader in dealing with climate change. And we all need to share a concern about Canada in the world.

I have often talked about the lessons I've learned after thirty years in politics, government, knocking on doors, making decisions, providing advice. Let me try to summarize a few.

First, the purpose of what we do is a better life for all Canadians, making sure that there are real opportunities for all our people, and that Canadians are doing what they can to make the world a safer, better place. The purpose is not to add to the power of a department, or the interest of one region or business, to say nothing of the ego of one person.

Second, while Canada will always be a country with regional differences, we must decide with courage what binds us together, what we owe one another. Having a vision doesn't mean that everything we aspire to can be accomplished overnight. Nothing worthwhile can. But having a compass allows for both baby and giant steps alike when conditions and opportunities permit.

Third, having a focused set of priorities with a coherent vision is better than trying to improve all the parts of government and all the problems at once.

Fourth, focus on outcomes, and don't be wedded to particular programs. Be clear about the goal, be flexible about the means. There will always be vested interests wedded to a particular program or institution. Don't let their rhetoric prevent you from asking, Is this really working, are we getting the outcomes we need and want?

Fifth, don't promise dozens of specific solutions for dozens of problems. There are always more good ideas than there is money. What seems simple from the outside is often more complex. And there are real partnerships required to make policy work.

Sixth, implementation and execution are key. Saying something and doing something are two different things. Governing well means delivering on commitments, with a capital D. And delivery is an art in itself, meaning experienced political leadership and talented public servants need to be involved in the development of policy as well as delivery.

Seventh, trust matters. It grows from getting the first six lessons right. You earn it by being open, transparent, visibly driving through on commitments, admitting mistakes when you make them, recalibrating when it is called for. Sticking to a vision. These are all things we try to teach our kids. We should expect politicians to live by these lessons as well.

Canada should be a place where all children go to school hungry for knowledge rather than hungry for food. That should be a key goal of our prosperity.

Our economy has done remarkably well in the last few years. But we can't just rest on our laurels. The world is a competitive place. Too many Canadians are being left behind. The rising tide has not lifted every boat. Governments need to sustain the high levels of prosperity that have been such a powerful feature of our society. Now is not a time to take the economy for granted. Yet the new Conservative government in Ottawa is doing just that – by literally buying off select groups with a grab-bag of tax credits and subsidies, none of which do much for long-run prosperity. An opportunity is being squandered by Ottawa today.

Canada's economy is in the balance. We can choose to build upon our impressive strengths and drive to a shared prosperity, or we can simply hope our recent successes continue. Complacency rarely works.

The biggest challenge we face today is the sense among a growing number of Canadians that they are on the outside looking in. Modern liberalism has wrestled for decades with this problem: how to use public policy to improve people's lives. With many successes to point to, Liberals believe government can keep making a difference. And they are right.

The gap between rich and poor is about people. It is also about regions and communities. In Newfoundland, for example, the collapse of the cod fishery wiped out a way of life for tens of thousands of people living in small communities. The closure of a mine, a fall in the price of wheat, a barrier to lumber exports – these are all realities that increase the divide between those Canadians who can seize the advantages of an innovative outward-looking economy and others who feel themselves falling behind.

Canada has adopted a variety of means to deal with these challenges: equalization payments to ensure a

rough equivalency of services like health care and education; regional development agencies to provide public
investment, marketing boards, supply management, crop
insurance, and agricultural income support programs;
the list goes on. Yet the problems persist. Rural communities feel threatened. Young people move away,
leaving families behind. Communities struggle to maintain services, to find and keep doctors and teachers.

The new conservative philosophy that says let's leave
it all to the marketplace and the provinces won't work
for a second, because it leaves people and communities
out of an impersonal equation. The work and focus of
the federal government needs to be revitalized, building
on the national commitment to learning, training, research,
and support for community economic development.
There is no one single magic bullet, but programs like
the earned income tax credit and a renewed commitment
to early childhood education will make a difference. So
will an energy strategy that builds on the possibilities of
wind power and smaller hydro projects. The digital
economy, with the right supports such as access to
broadband and the Internet, can actually lessen the
divide between urban and rural, between smaller communities and big cities, between east and west, north
and south.

I shall discuss later the steps we need to take to
bridge the continuing divide between Aboriginal and
non-Aboriginal Canadians. There are more divisions
public policy needs to address: the discrimination facing
Canadians with disabilities; persistent poverty and

homelessness in our urban centres; and a deep sense of loss and frustration in rural Canada and in smaller towns.

Each will require federal leadership. The barriers to opportunity need to be brought down. Most important, the national government has to show it understands the issues, and is prepared to stay committed and engaged. Canada stands alone among OECD countries in not having a national housing policy. Because of our federal nature, we shall have to work with provinces and cities, who have been playing a role. But there needs to be engagement.

In agriculture, we face a world where both Europe and the United States have made a conscious decision to subsidize and support farmers. So do we, but on a much smaller scale. With the continuing difficulty in trade talks, public policy has to accept the need for support. In the United States, our most important trading partner, more than half the seats in the U.S. Senate are controlled by less than 20 per cent of the population. This guarantees continuing battles on agricultural and resource trade with our American neighbours.

Farmers feed all Canadians. They are stewards of the land as well as producers of food. They can't be expected to continue farming if their income falls behind the costs of production. A market-based cost insurance plan, supported by both the provinces and the federal government, should be put in place to ensure the economic viability of the family farm.

Stephen Harper's agenda is to write the federal government out of the solutions. Nothing could be more short-sighted or ill-advised. It will mean the triumph of a "fend for yourself" society, in which communities and

people alike will be denied access to a federal government
that should be able to connect citizens.

The logic of a dynamic liberalism means a federal government that will invest in learning and opportunity
throughout the country, from Vancouver to Rimouski,
from Labrador to Toronto. A country that stops caring
about opportunities being shared fairly is very quickly a
country that stops mattering to its citizens. Harper talked
of building a firewall around one province, Alberta, so it
could keep itself away from the rest of the country.
Liberals have a different vision: a federal government that
will ensure the shared values of Canada are present across
the country.

We have to see economic and social investments
together, not in silos. The economy we are building needs
to work for all Canadians. Too many Canadians are still
poor. Badly designed and outdated income support systems
need the deepest reform.

The Toronto City Summit Alliance has ably pointed
this out in a recent report. For much of the country,
and for too many working Canadians, Employment
Insurance does not help. In Ontario, for example, a mere
27 per cent of those who lose their jobs are covered by
Employment Insurance. Many people are therefore forced
on to provincial welfare rolls for basic income support.
To qualify for welfare, people have to liquidate most of
their assets. Once on welfare, they will qualify for
certain benefits for themselves and their kids, such as
drug or dental, but taking a job means losing those
benefits. This is the classic poverty trap. The "downloading" from Employment Insurance to provincial

welfare programs is occurring at the same time as most provinces are financially stretched. Rapidly rising health and education costs add fuel to provincial claims of fiscal imbalance.

Canada needs an overhaul of the system of support for low-income Canadians, a change as important as the creation of unemployment insurance itself. Low-income families should be able to work and earn their way out of poverty, with income tax credits and enhanced child support. The earned income tax credit is working in many countries. It needs to work in Canada. The provinces and the federal government need to resolve the contradiction that people on welfare get drug and dental benefits while those working on minimum wage do not.

A new system of income support along these lines is not only required in a fair and just society, it is necessary for the growth and efficiency of the economy. It is where sound economic and progressive social policy meet. There should be no disincentives to work within our income and social support programs. Canadian citizens should have access to training and opportunity, not be needlessly stuck in poverty traps, or unable to make ends meet due to inadequate minimum wages or other supports.

Simplistic thinking sees social investment on one side of the equation and market forces on the other. This is antediluvian. Just as spending on physical infrastructure – roads, airports, gateways, and public transit – is critical for a modern, sustainable economy, so, too, the right investments in people, in their health, education, and well-being, can make us all more prosperous.

The Cart and the Horse

My ambition for Canada's economy is to build upon our remarkable strengths and successes in an effort to make the country truly innovative, dynamic, entrepreneurial, and global in orientation. This means celebrating and valuing wealth creation and entrepreneurialism in a way we have not traditionally done.

Canada also needs its governments to develop strategies for investment in people, research, and infrastructure to make individuals and firms as productive and competitive as they must be to thrive in a global economy.

We are blessed with one of the wealthiest, best-endowed, and most successful economies in the world. And yet we still have acute and persistent problems of poverty and exclusion. This should not be acceptable to Canadians. If we make the right choices in the coming years to secure our prosperity, we will equip ourselves with the means to achieve the truly just society that has eluded many Canadians for too long.

The most important drivers of an innovative society are its people. As I stated in my 2005 "Leader in Learning" report to the McGuinty government on higher education:

> ... education, research and innovation lie at the heart of our economy. This is not new. Every society has relied for its survival on the transfer of skills and abilities from generation to generation. What is new is the level and breadth of knowledge and skill required to make our way in the world. The wealth of Ontario now depends much more on the power of our brains.

Today our standard of living, and consequently our quality of life, depend on people having access to education that is on a par with the best in the world.

Education can unlock the world, for each of us as individuals and for Canada in the world.

Learning starts at birth, which is why we need to sustain and nurture working parents and their children. It carries through early childhood education. It is the focus for kids in schools, which in turn support communities, ensuring families have access to recreation, sports, and music. A country that takes learning seriously will take these investments seriously. We have both access and excellence challenges to meet at the post-secondary education level in the country. The cost of post-secondary education has been rising rapidly for years and shows no signs of abating. This obviously has implications for students from low-income families in particular. While the federal government has made some progress in improving access to post-secondary education, it needs to do more.

An overhaul of the federal student loans program is clearly needed. We need a program geared toward the living expenses and tuition costs of all students. We should reduce the contribution parents are expected to make to their children's education when determining eligibility for Canada Student Loans, as well as cut the interest rate on these loans. The federal government should also become a full funding partner in supporting priorities for labour market training, apprenticeship, research, and graduate education in a predictable and sustained way. The federal government needs to be doing a lot more to ensure access to post-secondary education.

As we all know, productivity growth is central to prosperity, and productivity is driven to a considerable extent when an economy generates innovative products and services, which are the fruits of research and development in firms, universities, and institutes. This is the excellence side of the equation.

Since the late 1990s, both the Chrétien and Martin governments have invested billions of dollars in university research infrastructure, granting councils, institutes like the National Research Council, and other organizations that constitute Canada's research infrastructure and "innovation chain." Given the often long-lead times needed for research to yield results, we are just now beginning to see the fruits of these investments.

The inaugural Harper budget was bereft of anything for research and innovation. That is a further indictment of the neoconservative economic orthodoxy that reigns in Ottawa today. Canada needs a research and innovation strategy, working in partnership with provinces, universities, research institutes, and the private sector, and building upon the investments made in recent years to ensure that we have world-class universities, globally competitive firms, and a highly productive workforce. What we don't need is rigid ideology that spouts free-market rhetoric but in fact fails to create the supportive environment that will allow innovative companies to succeed.

This strategy must include support for "pure science" as well as work that can go more quickly to the market. Experience tells us that there are still barriers to making the transfer from university research to commercial success. The link between the laboratory and the venture capitalist is by no means automatic or easy. Public policy needs to help make it happen.

Canada's big research universities tend to be located in our large cities, which are increasingly becoming the key economic and social organizing units of today. According to public-policy professor Richard Florida, winning cities today are those that have the most robust "Three Ts": *technology* – as measured by innovation and high-tech industry concentration; *talent* – as measured by the number of people in creative occupations, and *tolerance* – amenities and opportunities available for every possible lifestyle. Not surprisingly, some of Canada's cities score well on Florida's Three Ts index.

Developing robust innovation clusters – increasingly the major determinants of economic success in the global information economy – is another reason why we need to pay attention to university-industry-government alliances. The Medical and Related Sciences (MaRS) project, located near the University of Toronto, is a fine example of how such partnerships can work to the benefit of the firms, universities, and governments. It is a "condominium of ideas" – an incubator where science, finance, and entrepreneurship can support one another. We need more MaRS-type initiatives in this country to drive our innovation capacity, and there is a role for government here in making this happen.

Taking these ideas together – support for education, for a global vision, for student opportunity – led Jean Chrétien to create research chairs and a national network of scholarships. It led Paul Martin to announce the creation of Pearson Scholarships to support Canadians studying abroad and foreign students coming to Canada. We need to build on these programs with an ever-broader approach: a dramatic expansion of opportunity for Canadian students to enhance study abroad, and for international students to study and work in Canada, to match the imaginative and well-funded programs that now exist in the United States and Europe. We need to think bigger.

To education, we have to add culture. We have rich cultural traditions and artists that attract world attention and acclaim. But Canada's artistic and cultural organizations are in a constant state of financial crisis, not because their audiences are small, but because funding has never recovered from the major retrenchment that occurred in the 1990s. Given the role these organizations play in the life of our communities, this is profoundly short-sighted on the part of governments. Recently there have been some substantial investments in new buildings, which is all to the good, but does not address the ongoing need for a new approach.

Canada's cultural policy is falling behind the major changes underway in the world, and we need to get serious once again about what can be done. From my own work with the Royal Conservatory of Music and the Toronto Symphony Orchestra, I saw talent, potential, and opportunities. I would like to see matching funds apply to operating, capital, and endowment funds, so that the government can more clearly provide incentives to philanthropy. This would be in addition to enhanced core funding provided by federal, provincial, and city governments. A thriving arts scene is an expression of thriving communities and tangibly boosts local economies.

The productivity of an economy is dependent on infrastructure. Much of Canada's infrastructure – roads, bridges, sewer systems, etc. – was built decades ago and needs to be replaced or refurbished. While the fiscal deficit has been addressed, Canada still suffers an infrastructure investment deficit. A recent Statistics Canada study looked at federal, provincial, and municipal infrastructure and concluded that wastewater facilities had 63 per cent of their useful life behind them, while roads and highways were at 59 per cent, sewer systems at 52 per cent, and bridges at 49 per cent. This is a serious, long-term issue that requires a sustained, and visionary, commitment.

Canada needs a comprehensive "green" infrastructure renewal strategy, bringing together all levels of government in common purpose. In this age of global integration of manufacturing and supply chains, low inventories, and just-in-time delivery, the economy needs reliable, environmentally friendly infrastructure that facilitates the efficient transportation of goods and people. Canada's transportation infrastructure, including ports and border crossings, needs improving to enable goods to move more quickly and efficiently within our national borders and between Canada and the United States. We also require more and better mass transit systems in our cities to combat gridlock, conserve energy, reduce greenhouse gas emissions, and make our cities more livable and appealing.

Federal-provincial partnership investments in projects that would help us to reach our Kyoto objectives, including alternative energy projects such as wind power and hydro and carbon sequestration, must be pursued. An east-west power grid to help ensure adequate carriage and energy security for Canadian citizens and businesses could be the modern equivalent of the transcontinental railway.

Partnering with provinces and municipalities on strategic investments in green infrastructure is a long-term proposition that benefits more than one generation. These are progressive investments that will help keep our national economy humming and ensure that prosperity and competitiveness is on an environmentally sustainable footing.

More than 40 per cent of Canada's gross domestic product (GDP) is derived from trade. Ensuring barrier-free access to existing markets, and aggressively targeting and capitalizing on new opportunities, is therefore vital to our economic interests. As alluded to earlier, the combination of U.S. protectionism, cracks in the U.S. economy, and historic trade and investment opportunities in the emerging economic giants – particularly China and India – present both challenges and opportunities for Canada's trade and investment policy. We need to seize the opportunities in these huge, developing markets and diversify our trading and investment relationships. Yet we have seen a worrying decline in Canadian sales and investment into China, at a time when most other advanced economies are aggressively moving into this massive, dynamic economy, which has grown at more than 9 per cent per annum for more than two decades.

Canada has a truly historic opportunity here that we cannot miss. Our country has unique comparative strengths in India and China that we can draw upon to succeed there, in particular our large Chinese and Indian diaspora communities and our Pacific orientation through the province of British Columbia. But we have to utilize these advantages better than we have to date. Canada needs a broader China and India trade and investment strategy, and we need it yesterday.

Related to this is the fact that the great strengths of Canada's economy, society, and people are not well understood around the world. Canada still tends to be viewed abroad as an "old economy" country. This has negative repercussions for investment and for attracting highly qualified people to Canada. It is an image problem we need to take concerted action to correct.

This requires branding Canada to align our international image with the Canadian reality of today. *The Economist* magazine helped us in this regard three years ago with its "Cool Canada" cover – and articles that debunked some of the lingering myths about Canada and its economy. But our governments need to take up this challenge more forcefully. We need to promote and market internationally the dynamic, innovative global information economy – and our highly educated and skilled workforce – that is the heart of today's Canada. We also need to start bragging more about our world-leading social infrastructure, which has some elements, such as our single-payer health-care system, that gives firms a huge competitive cost advantage relative to the United States. Our rich cultural amenities should also be part of this branding effort.

Branding, promoting, and marketing are not frivolities in today's global economy, where competition for investment and people is fierce. If we have an image problem, we need to fix it now.

Over the next five years, immigration will account for 100 per cent of net labour force growth in Canada. Yet business immigration has been declining, in part due to our immigration system, which does not put a priority on this class of immigrants. Moreover, our economy loses $4 billion to $5 billion per year due to the well-known credential recognition problem many immigrants face once they get here: skilled and talented immigrants whose credentials obtained abroad are not recognized by governing and accreditation bodies in Canada. Equally important, small- and medium-sized businesses are facing a shortage of skilled tradespeople. This is also due in part to failings in our immigration system – our immigration authorities need to put a higher priority on aligning labour market demand with the supply of skilled people awaiting approval in our system. That means changing the points system.

Canada's immigration policy and system is critical to our economic prosperity, more than ever over the next number of years with our demographic challenges. But the system is not working well enough and needs some significant reforms to ensure we get the talented and skilled people we need. Canada will be in a fierce competition with other advanced countries for the world's skilled immigrants in the coming years, given the common demographic realities that exist across the western industrial world. Ottawa needs to get beyond the platitudes and fix our immigration system now before it further hampers Canadian prosperity by discouraging immigrants from coming here, while simultaneously wasting the talents of many of those that are already in this country.

Speaking with new Canadians across the country, one gets a powerful impression of mixed emotions. Canada is a great country, but family reunification takes too much time. The process of application itself is a challenge. Integration is difficult when faced with barriers. We need to listen to these voices.

My optimism and ambition regarding Canada's economic prospects no doubt stem from my own experiences. Because I have governed through some of the most difficult economic times the country has recently faced – where we stared down intractable problems of recession, high and rising unemployment, and all that follows – today's Canada looks very strong indeed.

During my time at Queen's Park, governments of all political stripes across Canada and around the industrial world found that they had little ability to pull the economy out of the slump on their own. We could help weather the storm. We could not easily change the weather. For governments, if your nation's economy is trade-dependent, as is Canada's, pulling out of recessions can be harder than staying out of them. This is another reason why sustaining strong economic growth and putting in place the policies to promote a dynamic economy that creates wealth must be priority one.

One of Canada's greatest exports to the United States, the late John Kenneth Galbraith, once caustically remarked, "Wealth is not without its advantages, and the case to the contrary, although it has often been made, has never proved widely persuasive." For Galbraith, wealth creation was vitally important and entirely compatible with progressive government. Not all in this country would agree; some people are downright hostile to wealth creation, the entrepreneurial ethic, and business generally.

I am with Galbraith on this point. The "progressive idea" cannot be pursued absent a strong, productive, dynamic, and growing economy that creates wealth. There is no contradiction between having a modern social agenda for the country, while valuing economic growth and putting a premium on prosperity, competition, wealth creation, and entrepreneurialism. In fact, a social agenda and economic dynamism are self-reinforcing in the global information economy.

It is a lot easier to achieve this approach with budgets in balance as well. Canada came out of the Second World War with a huge deficit. We paid it down in the 1950s and 1960s, and returned to borrowing in the 1970s. This became a serious challenge in the 1990s. I know whereof I speak.

Getting the books into balance, and surplus, was a significant achievement of the Chrétien/Martin years.

With higher revenues on all fronts, and tough decisions on spending and transfers, the fiscal position of the federal government was transformed.

We should keep it that way.

Successive Liberal governments have paid off more than $60 billion in federal debt so that today the federal debt-to-GDP ratio stands at just more than 30 per cent, its lowest level in decades. It makes sense to pay down debt when the economy is exhibiting strong growth, as has been the case for the last number of years, and as is anticipated in the immediate future. When we can afford to make additional payments on the national mortgage, we should do so.

Taxes are not a matter of theology. They are practical realities. We need to pay them to make sure we can provide the services that people want and need. But they have to be structured in a way that ensures both fairness and a productive economy. The Harper government's vaunted GST cut might seem to be clever politics, but it is poor economics. This is one area where Harper has managed the unthinkable – he has produced a consensus among his fellow economists. Almost all agree the GST cut, paid for with an increase in income taxes, is terrible economics. Though the GST may irritate people, Canadians benefit little, and are given few choices when it is reduced. They must spend money to get the benefit, which obviously favours those who have more income and can spend more. It is, therefore, regressive.

Broad-based income tax cuts are a much better way to go, because they promote the long-term prosperity of the economy and give Canadians more choices – to invest the benefit in their children's education, or their homes, to save it for their retirement, or to spend it. An income tax cut helps low- and middle-income families and can reduce income disparities. It is progressive and will have positive, long-term effects on the economy in terms of investment, productivity, and savings. No less an authority than the federal Department of Finance has stated that an income tax cut is three times as good for the economy as a GST cut.

Canadians and Canadian business, particularly small and medium-sized businesses, also need a simplified tax system that reduces the duplication between different levels of government. Disentangling Canada's increasingly Byzantine tax system is long overdue. Federal and provincial governments need to collaborate energetically on this task. Yet these days we hear almost nothing out of Ottawa about tax simplification. Judging by the national tax debate today, one would conclude that our existing system is optimum, requiring some tweaking of rates and a few more tax credits to encourage allegedly desirable human behaviour. Nothing could be further from the truth.

As heretical as this may sound to some, corporate taxes must also be a concern for modern progressives. In a global economy where capital is mobile, countries are in perpetual competition for business investment. Canada is no exception. We simply must accept that taxes play a big role in private sector investment decisions. This is not some ideological mantra.

Governments must ensure that our corporate taxes are internationally competitive. Today, at the federal level, we must keep them in line with key jurisdictions. This is not a "race to the bottom" agenda. It will, in fact, help ensure that Canada stays on top in the global competition for investment, from both foreign and Canadian companies.

We must also improve our tax system so that it has the right incentives to help us achieve a more sustainable economy and society. In facing up to the Kyoto challenge, we have made minimal use of our taxation system to send price signals to help consumers, businesses, and the economy to adjust to the need to reduce greenhouse gases. If done wisely, using the tax system and prices to achieve a more sustainable economy will make us more competitive, as we encourage greater energy efficiency in our economy. We also need to encourage the use of energy-efficient appliances, building standards, alternative energy sources, and the use of more fuel-efficient cars. Combined with income tax cuts, this can be done in a revenue-neutral way. We can improve the environment without hampering productivity.

Small and medium-sized companies are the engine of economic growth and job creation – they account for 50 per cent of our economy and are responsible for 70 per cent of new job creation. The federal government needs to work to keep this engine humming along, encourage entrepreneurialism, and assist companies to penetrate global markets.

Regulation is consistently identified as one of the great impediments to small-business success. Governments need to regulate smarter and be much more attentive to the effect of regulations. This must be a critical and ongoing preoccupation. Getting our regulatory framework right, and making more use of on-line services for business and consumers, can have huge economic payoffs.

The food industry is a good example. We have an innovative and productive world-leading agri-food industry in Canada. But our associated review and approval processes are holding the industry back. Our Food and Drug Act is simply not keeping up with worldwide scientific advances. It cries out for a consultative, legislative renewal process, and then proper funding of our regulatory agencies, so that timeliness, consumer education, and environmental protection needs can all be met. This affects large, medium, and small businesses.

The massive federal procurement budget also offers significant opportunities for small business. We should be aiming to reduce the complexity of the process, and ensure all businesses can compete on the basis of quality, timeliness, and price. The system requires greater transparency, simplicity, and efficiency, which would open up opportunities for small and medium-sized businesses to grow and create jobs in communities across Canada.

We need to create a culture and legal framework that supports risk. We are a belt-and-suspenders kind of people. This has its advantages, but it also means we don't do enough to encourage the kind of entrepreneurial spirit that is critical for innovation.

Startup companies need access to capital, which means both equity and debt. Our capital markets are still too small and divided. Our tax policies are not aggressive enough.

These issues will need to be addressed. Taking wealth creation seriously is an essential part of a new agenda for the country.

Above all, we need to see these elements as an interconnected whole. The attitude that business success is unimportant to the fight against poverty is as outdated as the notion that health care is a purely social issue. Sharing opportunity is as much about enhancing productivity as it is about "social justice." These issues have to be understood as part of a linked approach. The progressive agenda is about social cohesion *and* a dynamic economy, about bringing people together in a shared enterprise: a self-confident and prosperous Canada.

CHAPTER FOUR

A Wider Vision:
What We Owe One Another

A WIDER VISION WILL BREAK DOWN THE ARTIFICIAL barriers between economic, social, and environmental policy. The common goal of the enterprise called "public policy" is the well-being of each and every citizen of Canada. We can't ensure that well-being by keeping things as they are.

Capital, labour, and public policy have to be more fluid in adjusting to rapid change and intense international competition. Governments can no longer take five years to mull over a problem and consider amendments to old rules that were forged for a different era. Instead, they have to be agile, and their goal has to be to ensure that businesses and people are mobile – that they have the freedom and the resilience to respond to new opportunities and to absorb unexpected risks.

Today we frustrate innovation and short-change ourselves by trapping people in situations they cannot change.

- Business feels trapped by outmoded regulations and tax policy.
- Working people feel trapped by the lack of access to retraining and the lack of job ladders that foster learning on the job.
- Young people are trapped by the lack of entry-level jobs and good apprenticeship or work experience opportunities. They are trapped into debt by having to spend ten years getting enough education to qualify for the good jobs.
- Immigrants are trapped because their credentials are not recognized.
- People on welfare are trapped by the way social programs penalize progress and saving.
- Women are trapped by the lack of child care and the requirement to work.
- Aboriginals are trapped by the social distress in their families and communities.

I think that Canadians are yearning for a vision that focuses on the opportunities and challenges we are creating for our children and grandchildren.

Ken Dryden's leadership in developing a new national child-care program was visionary, and we need to get it back on track. Early learning and care, ensuring we have a national child-care program to catch up to Quebec and countries like Belgium, Denmark, and France, is the very best collective investment we can make to our future as a nation.

High-quality, developmentally enriched, and universally available child care must be part of our vision for lifelong learning, social inclusion, and supports for the employed and employable.

Nothing better illustrates the Harper approach of survival-of-the-fittest, go-it-alone philosophy than their misnamed policies on child care. To use the words *universal* and *plan* in naming their $1,200-per-year scheme is a cynical effort to confuse the public. Worse yet, to use the Trojan Horse of "choice" as a way to eliminate choice, including the best choice for parents and guardians, is devastating in its intent. Harper provides us with a stark contrast between his version of rugged individualism and what Liberals seek as the appropriate balance between the individual and community. Some things require that we build them together. I can't make clean air or clean water for myself and my family. Nor can I build great public education or health care or child care by myself.

Like health care, I think the federal government can be a co-funder with the provinces and provide enough of the resources to play a "a guiding principles" and accountability role.

Investing in the early years must be the springboard for learning for life. Great child care provides the basis, through learning through play, for the enjoyment of learning.

Learning is always in the air. Five million kids are in our elementary and secondary schools across Canada, and two million students are enrolled in our fine universities and colleges.

My recent experience as a commissioner for post-secondary education was a wonderful opportunity to reconnect to the challenges and opportunities facing all levels of our education systems in Canada. My work, and the subsequent and countless opportunities to talk with people across the country, has confirmed my view that Canadians want prosperity and fairness to go hand in hand, that sound economic policy is not an end in itself but must serve a better future for all Canadians, not just a few. Our prosperity must have purpose. Education and learning throughout one's life is key to a healthier and a more productive life. And we need to ensure that those who are disadvantaged, through no fault of their own, have much greater opportunities to participate in our formal learning institutions.

It is clear that child poverty, high student dropout rates, and illiteracy are enemies of prosperity. The inability to read and write represents a huge obstacle to participating in the best our country has to offer. StatsCan reports that more than 42 per cent of Canadians aged sixteen to sixty-five do not possess the skills to meet everyday reading requirements. StatsCan has also produced a recent report noting that for every 1 per cent rise in the average literacy level of Canadians, $18 billion will be added to the GDP. Fairness and prosperity, a hand-in-hand proposition.

A great post-secondary education is the best ticket for a healthy and prosperous future. It is also clear that the other bookend of lifelong learning – early childhood education – is the springboard for all that follows. My three children have taught me over the past many years about the marvellous capacity of children to learn new things, about how critical it is to foster a love of, and skills for, learning from the very beginning.

Canadians are rightly proud of our medicare system. They want to improve on the basic concept, not turn it upside down and go the private funding route of the United States. Our medicare and public health systems have helped ensure one of the healthiest populations in the world, and have meant that individuals and families are not bankrupted by the costs of needed health care. The system has challenges, as we all know. But it remains among the highest quality and most cost-effective in the world.

Indeed, this "social program" is also a competitive advantage for Canada. Automobile companies and other industries are citing it as a key factor in their decisions to locate and invest in Canada, creating many good jobs for Canadians along the way. It would be wrong to fritter away this huge advantage, or let the challenges it faces defeat us.

Canadians want health coverage that is of good quality, that is reasonably accessible, and that is timely. Above all they want to enjoy good health – an excellent quality of life is what the debate is all about.

Talking to ordinary citizens, health-care providers, and administrators, and having been responsible for the largest health-care system in the country when I was premier of Ontario, a few things stand out for me as key areas of focus for the federal government:

- pharmaceutical drugs, especially how to pay for the cost of catastrophic drug coverage for all Canadians
- an effective wait-times strategy, including applying the latest technologies to improving the management of care ("e-health")
- strengthening the Canada Health Act by embedding performance reporting to the public into the act, using comparable indicators and common benchmarks so that governments themselves are more accountable and transparent in the way they spend public funds and in the performance they achieve
- health human resources: Shortages of doctors, nurses, lab technicians, physiotherapists, and other health professionals need to be addressed on a national basis, working in concert with the provinces and territories. Too many people can't access a family doctor, radiologists are in short supply, and nursing faces large retirements. Meanwhile, we have a cumbersome, inefficient approach to recognizing the credentials of foreign-trained health professionals.
- healthy Canadians: We need to improve chronic disease prevention and management. Childhood obesity has shot up, and needs addressing. We also

need to work collaboratively to close the health gap
that presently exists for Aboriginal Canadians

As our population ages, as we live longer, and as technology improves, we can only avoid overwhelming our
health system through better management: between
governments, between institutions, and by each of us as
citizens. It also includes better management of chronic
diseases such as diabetes, asthma, and congestive heart
failure. Ensuring that patients become partners in their
own care will mean that these conditions can be controlled and do not become crises for individuals that
collectively can overwhelm acute services. A strong
primary health-care system is vital to the focus on
chronic disease management and prevention.

High-quality, universally available health care is not
simply a citadel to be protected from assault. We have to
keep improving the system. It is not an icon. It is a
service whose quality and availability are an important
reflection of the values we share as citizens. And it is a
service that can get better.

Pharmaceutical drugs are a costly but increasingly
necessary component of health care. We spend more on
drugs in Canada every year than we do on physician services. New drugs are reducing the need for certain types
of surgery and have improved the quality of life and survival rates for patients. Some of these new agents, though,
are extraordinarily expensive, and having to pay for them
out of pocket would bankrupt most of us. That is why
such costs are referred to as "catastrophic."

It is this very phenomenon of such financial devastation that led an earlier generation to establish medicare in the first place. The idea was to "pool risk" and use the collective wealth of society to ensure all Canadian citizens would be covered and not have to worry about ill health devastating a family's finances.

Unlike physician and hospital services, drugs do not come under the Canada Health Act. Nevertheless, all provinces and territories have introduced some form of drug coverage for some portion of their population. Other citizens rely on employer-funded drug benefit programs to cover the cost of needed pharmaceuticals.

But this patchwork has a few critical gaps. Many Canadians get no coverage at all. In the Atlantic provinces, there is no coverage for "catastrophic drugs." Other provinces have chosen in some instances not to cover certain drugs that may provide the only hope for patients.

That leaves some of our citizens having to choose literally between sacrificing their health and financial devastation. Like the earlier generation that founded medicare, we need to ensure today that that situation does not continue.

When I was premier of Ontario, the government started the Trillium Drug Plan. I am proud of that achievement. It has saved lives and, on a practical level, prevented great personal hardship. I believe that the time has come for a national catastrophic drug plan, which I would call the Maple Leaf Plan. Previous Liberal governments, following the recommendation of the National Forum on Health, committed to a National

Pharmacare Program. But the complexity, scale, and political challenges meant this well-intentioned effort never got off the ground. My sense is that a more focused effort, which zeroes in on the catastrophic cost and builds on provincial plans, would have a far better prospect of success.

There is much talk these days of a "fiscal imbalance" where the revenues of the federal government are compared to those of provincial governments. The prevailing assumption seems to be that the federal government should simply hand over its "excess surplus" through increased transfers, or vacate tax room. Those ideas may have some merit. But we should also be thinking about using the resources of the central government to bolster one of our most important social programs and relieve a difficult burden from provinces.

A number of provinces have already voiced their support for the notion of the feds taking on responsibility for catastrophic drug coverage, and indeed proposed it to the federal government in the negotiations over the most recent Health Accord.

I envision a single, public, nationally insured catastrophic drug plan with provincial opt in or out. A common formulary would be established using the common drug review, and would be based on an evaluation of evidence and cost-effectiveness. It would allow us to fund existing as well as new expensive medications that exceed a specified threshold cash value. Creation of a national formulary will improve predictability, portability, and coverage for new and expensive drugs as they emerge in the marketplace.

For administrative simplicity, the Maple Leaf Plan could be built on existing provincial programs and be administered through an *auditable* government-to-government reimbursement scheme for eligible patients. Eligibility would be based on a national set of rules related to cost-sharing. Provinces with existing catastrophic schemes would simply have reimbursed those cases that fit the thresholds and the formulary of the federal program. There are many efficiencies in our current public patchwork of drug coverage that could be achieved with a national catastrophic formulary, not least of which is the notion of one national standard of evidence and cost-effectiveness for very expensive drugs.

Many other details would have to be worked out collaboratively with provinces and territories. It would have to be costed, where thresholds, eligibility, and cost-sharing were adjusted to ensure affordability. But pooling risk, pooling cost, and establishing a single national formulary are cost-effectiveness measures in themselves, like the single-payer medicare system.

The issue of lengthy wait times in our health system for key procedures has been a top concern of Canadians the last number of years. In the recent First Ministers' Health Accord, governments in all jurisdictions agreed to work together to achieve improvements in five priority areas: cardiac care, cancer treatment, joint replacement, diagnostic imaging, and sight restoration. Through collaboration, notable progress has been made to establish benchmarks in each of these areas.

Governments have also committed to establishing comparable indicators to measure progress against the benchmarks, and comparable indicators of access to health-care professionals. With the benchmarks and indi- cators set, governments are clearly working hard to achieve these benchmarks for timely care by December 2007. But we need to keep a focus on transparent public reporting on wait times.

I strongly endorse this practice of establishing benchmarks, developing common indicators of progress against those standards, and setting target dates for their achievement. It is also important that all of this information be made public so that citizens can track progress, make comparisons, and see that the huge amounts of public investment that go into supporting medicare are being well used and that continuous quality improvement is occurring.

Achieving a higher level of confidence on the part of Canadians is essential if medicare is to be sustainable in the long run. But there is much more to be done to get us where we need to be in terms of timeliness, quality, and sustainability in our Canadian health-care system.

The Chaoulli decision by the Supreme Court has made it clear that there is a legal as well as moral obligation to ensure that the public system not require waits for care that can hurt people's health.

The Conservatives made much of their "Care Guarantee" in the last election, calling it one of their top-five priorities. The notion of the "guarantee" is that if care is not obtained within the time specified in the benchmarks, special measures will be taken, up to and including flying patients to other jurisdictions to receive timely care.

But to date, the Conservative government has done precisely nothing to support provinces in achieving this "promise" to impose on them a higher level of "guaranteed care." And they are actually attempting to claim that the funds for health care committed by the previous Liberal government are sufficient for provincial governments to implement the care guarantee.

Declaring a thing to be so does not make it so, especially when the responsibilities for delivering such care fall under provincial jurisdiction.

Offering a "guarantee" to achieve something in someone else's jurisdiction, while offering no additional resources, plans, or processes for getting there, makes no sense. There has been much fuss made in the media about Harper being a man who keeps his promises. He has, in fact, broken his word on health care, Canadians' top priority.

Many reports have also called on the federal government to increase its support for e-health, including the development of wait-list management tools, electronic health records, telehealth, and better performance reporting systems. The Health Council of Canada regards the use of electronic patient records as one of the top priorities for improving the quality, safety, and timeliness of care.

At present in Canada, most medical records are paper-based and not readily accessible to support a patient moving across the continuum of professionals in today's more team-based approach to care. Electronic health records ensure that authorized health professionals can securely access a patient's confidential medical record at the time of care. Electronic wait-list management tools are also extremely helpful in the efficient management of wait lists. Telehealth can reduce the need for costly travel. And information management systems allow for timely reporting on outcomes and performance.

In the late 1990s, I had the chance to serve on the Quality Committee of the University Health Network in Toronto. It was eye-opening. Mistakes happen in institutions big and small. But when they happen in hospitals, people can get sicker and even lose their lives. Improving quality and quality systems are not frills. They are essential to good health.

Provinces have consistently faced challenges in paying for these needed systems. It is one area where such non-intrusive federal assistance would be warmly welcomed by provinces and territories.

In First Nations communities, much greater use can and should be made of telehealth to help manage high rates of diabetes, reduce the need for expensive travel to care centres, and allow individuals to continue with daily life with their families in their own communities. Supporting adequate broadband access is crucial to enabling such telehealth services, and was a key commitment in the Kelowna Accord.

The Canada Health Act was designed and passed into law under the stewardship of Monique Bégin when she was the federal minister of health and welfare. It is one of the great acts in our history, and for many has come to symbolize medicare. Its five principles of universality, public administration, portability, accessibility, and comprehensiveness, and its prohibitions against user fees and extra-billing, have helped to protect and sustain the original spirit and values behind the creation of the system.

We live now in an era of greater public expectations around accountability and transparency for performance and the wise use of public funds. If we are to endorse the public administration of health services, then we need a higher measure of public accountability for performance. In the private sector, as well, where shareholder interests are concerned, much higher degrees of transparency and accurate public reporting are expected today.

Successive First Ministers' Health Accords have, following much intense debate, included commitments for reporting to the public in their jurisdictions on performance in key areas. Several provinces and the federal government have also created Quality Councils to report annually on health system performance. The public has welcomed such developments. Canadians want to know that their dollars are being well spent and that the system is improving and addressing problem areas systematically. There is good momentum on this agenda. It is a trend that deserves to be consolidated for the long-term.

These health accords are important. But they do not have the same force or symbolism as legislation. We should strengthen the Canada Health Act by adding an accountability principle that would compel public reporting on health system performance, using comparable indicators and common data standards. This would become a sixth principle of the Act.

Giving accountability the force of law and making it a condition of transfer ensures that we do not slide back in any jurisdiction because a government one day decides it is too onerous or costly a process or because their performance is not what they want it to be.

We would be making this change in conjunction with the new federal investments in health care, which would help provinces and territories to improve system performance and afford the information management systems that make reporting a much more straightforward task.

Canada faces shortages in the number of health professionals in our system. Shortages of nurses, family doctors, anesthesiologists, and other specialists put pressures on the system, contribute to bottlenecks, and thereby add to the problem of wait times for procedures. Provinces are actively moving to increase the number of spaces available in schools of nursing, medicine, etc. But it takes eight years to develop a medical specialist, for example. And we can't wait that long.

Efforts have begun in some quarters to support more innovative use of the professionals currently in the system and maximize the use of skills that health professionals have. For example, general practice in rural areas could be assisted through the expanded use of nurse practitioners. Use of nurse anesthesiologists is widely practised in other jurisdictions, and could be a highly effective way of dealing with a serious current shortage. Patient safety and quality of care would, of course, have to be paramount in any such initiatives.

We see far too many unnecessary, preventable cancers develop because screening is not occurring on the scale it should, because of the lack of endoscopy profession-

als and gastroenterologists. In the U.K. and at Kaiser Permanente in the United States, nurses are currently providing these endoscopy services. We need to learn from these innovators.

What we lack in Canada right now are jurisdiction-wide initiatives for such extended practice schemes for nurses and primary-care practitioners to take on roles that will help with the current pressures within the delivery system.

We also need to standardize processes across the country for the recognition of the credentials of immigrant health professionals. This, too, would help greatly in expediting our ability to hire the professionals we need to deliver care in our communities. It will require extensive collaboration with the provinces and self-regulating professions. But it has to happen.

Canadians are, compared to citizens of other countries, quite healthy. Sixty per cent of the population assesses their own health as very good to excellent. Average life expectancy is increasing, and is one of the highest in the world at eighty-two years for women and seventy-seven years for men. Important public health measures are being taken to supply vaccines for children with the National Immunization Strategy. Anti-smoking strategies seems to have taken hold, as smoking rates continue to go down.

But there are clouds on this horizon. With an aging population we face increasing levels of certain chronic diseases. More than 60 per cent of health-care costs are now dedicated to dealing with chronic diseases. The Health Council of Canada estimates an annual $80 billion-per-year price tag in health-care costs and lost productivity. So this burden is an issue for health system sustainability, the economy, as well as individual quality of life.

Obesity among children has increased markedly in Canada in the last two decades. Our kids are engaging in too many sedentary activities, and not eating as well as they should. Most adults could also afford to walk more, drive less, and eat healthier. That's why we should bring back ParticiPACTION. Health inequalities between regions and population groups are also an issue. There has been a persistent gap between the health of Aboriginal populations and other Canadians that has to be tackled. Mental health remains too much a "hidden" disease.

The harm from the production, sale, and use of illicit drugs, psychoactive substances, is a blight in many poor neighbourhoods, such as Vancouver's Lower East Side and other urban centres. It must be recognized as a health issue, not just a law enforcement matter. I favour a balanced approach that includes harm reduction, prevention, and support to individuals to get off drugs on the user-demand side, as well as effective enforcement targeting the illegal trade.

The track record on such issues as quitting smoking, childhood immunization, and public health readiness shows that governments, working in partnership, can make tangible progress on complicated problems. A key ingredient here is that while governments alone cannot do the job, they are a part of the solution, not part of the problem.

The long-term sustainability of medicare and our health system depends on our making headway on these population health issues. Nothing is dearer to Canadians than good health. Alongside education, it should be at the top of the agenda for Canada's federal government, and indeed all governments. Government can't produce good health on its own, but it certainly can and should create the conditions in which it can flourish.

I have learned a few things about health care. The first is that the public need and demand for it is very great. The second is that the problems, bottlenecks, and delays are solvable, but they are not just about money. They are partly caused by turf wars, inefficient practices, too much attachment to "how things have always been done." The third is that the main determinants of good health lie outside the health-care system: good housing, good nutrition, good jobs all have a lot to do with how well we are. It's a lot easier to spend money on treatment than on prevention: Mr. Jones with his heart condition doesn't want a lecture on smoking and diet.

Mental health and public health are the poor cousins of the health-care debate. This is where federal leadership can play a role. It's precisely because the federal government doesn't run provincial hospitals that it should be able to look more broadly.

Finally, the federal government is constitutionally responsible for Aboriginal health care. Why not make this a model? One suspects it is not: big bureaucracies removed from communities, no clear focus on outcomes, these are hardly state-of-the-art approaches. We can and should improve.

A vision crafted by a single person, even with the power of position, is useless. We must seek a shared vision, one that is coherent, one with clarity of responsibility for funding and delivery, one that is intellectually and emotionally owned by those asked to breathe life into public policy where it counts, in the neighbourhoods of our nation.

We make our political choices in the context of change happening around us. Canadians are getting older, which will have a profound impact on everything government does. We know for certain that the demands on the health-care system will grow. We are the beneficiaries of a technological change that helps transform fatal illnesses into chronic conditions. We shall live longer. We shall be living farther away from our families.

Health-care costs will grow, although the changes and improvements I am suggesting should help. Seniors will be increasingly concerned about their incomes, their independence, and the quality of their lives.

Compulsory retirement is an idea whose time has come and gone. There are, of course, jobs and occupations that become more difficult to perform as people get older, but these are fewer in number than a generation ago. With a more flexible retirement will also come the understanding that it is not an absolute concept.

The baby-boom generation of which I am a member has defined much of public policy for fifty years. A less deferential age will naturally see a continuing questioning of authority and a rejection of a sense of "being handled." That's why public policy needs to concentrate on supports for independent living and opportunities for participation. This will involve controversy, but will be positive.

We need a national discussion about what the government should be doing to ensure that there will be someone there to care for seniors when they need support. So far, the focus has been on income security and health care. But we have neglected the infrastructure of personal supports offered by family and community. Will it be robust enough to handle the coming expansion of the frail elderly?

Judith Maxwell, a leading public-policy thinker, wrote about this in the May 2006 issue of *Policy Options* magazine:

In the 1960s, Canadians were so embarrassed by the rates of poverty among older Canadians that they implemented a wide range of retirement income supports – ranging from a guaranteed income supplement for the poorest, to Old Age Security, to tax breaks for retirement savings by people with discretionary income. Within a short time, poverty rates for elders plummeted, and remain low forty years later. This was a policy triumph, even though the poorest of the poor remain vulnerable. Our limited capacity for social and health care for this generation is already sorely stretched, even before the baby boomers reach that stage of life. [We need a social care system.]

What do social care systems look like? An OECD study by [Jane] Jenson and [Stéphane] Jacobzone shows that countries have made different choices, often combining several options:

- Some have established social insurance – contributory savings plans to ensure that elders will have access to good care when they need it, either in an institution or in their own home. (Quebec, where the population is aging rapidly, is considering a form of "autonomy insurance" like this.)
- Others have invested in state services – assisted housing, home care.
- Some provide care allowances to the elder so that she can pay for the supports she needs – whether that help comes from a family member or someone else.
- Some have adjusted pension systems to give pension credits for years spent caring for a relative.

Here in Canada, we can rely more on high quality non-profit organizations to deliver community services. Community resource centres which provide early assessments of need and then make referrals to caregiving services are an example that comes to mind. Other non-profits can provide assisted housing, and could do more if they had better access to capital. In every case, the motivation is to support family reciprocity: there is no perfect substitute for the care from a family member. But we must not make the mistake of assuming that unpaid family members can do it all.

All Canadians can rely on a solid foundation of universal health care coverage. But we cannot expect the over-stretched health care system to expand to perform all the personal care services that are so essential to people in fragile health.

Maxwell is rightly raising these issues, since they speak to the reality of an aging society and a population with a different set of values and concerns.

Which leads to a final point: the style of governing. Canadians look to leaders for answers, but creative governing actually means something else. Citizens also want to be engaged, and this implies a new approach to governing. It can't be top down, it can't be authoritarian. It can't be secretive. It involves sharing information, listening, partnering with people who know better, and really engaging with Canadians about the nature of the choices we face.

CHAPTER   FIVE

———◆———

Sustainability

A NEW LENS HAS TO BE APPLIED TO OUR VISION OF the future: sustainability. Like millions around the world, Canadians have become increasingly aware that industrial progress over the last several centuries has come with a price – the alarming imbalance between humankind and nature.

From the pollution of air and water to urban sprawl, from the spread of the Sahara to the overfishing of the Earth's oceans, the world is pursuing wealth creation at the expense of the things we have in common.

It does not have to be this way. There is a way of meeting the globe's material needs and wants without plundering the planet. But it is a way that requires us to put broader interests first and to plan for the long-term.

Speaking of climate change, which is certainly the

great environmental challenge of our time, British prime minister Tony Blair had this to say on September 14, 2004:

> From the start of the industrial revolution more than 200 years ago, developed nations have achieved ever greater prosperity and higher living standards. But through this period our activities have come to affect our atmosphere, oceans, geology, chemistry and biodiversity.
>
> What is now plain is that the emission of greenhouse gases, associated with industrialization and strong economic growth from a world population that has increased sixfold in 200 years, is causing global warming at a rate that began as significant, has become alarming and is simply unsustainable in the long-term. And by long-term I do not mean centuries ahead. I mean within the lifetime of my children certainly; and possibly within my own. And by unsustainable, I do mean a phenomenon causing problems of adjustment. I mean a challenge so far-reaching in its impact and irreversible in its destructive power, that it alters radically human existence.
>
> The problem and let me state it frankly at the outset – is that the challenge is complicated politically by two factors. First, its likely effect will not be felt to its full extent until after the time for the political decisions that need to be taken, has passed. In other words, there

is a mismatch in timing between the environmental and electoral impact. Secondly, no one nation alone can resolve it. It has no definable boundaries. Short of international action commonly agreed and commonly followed through, it is hard even for a large country to make a difference on its own.

But there is no doubt that the time to act is now. It is now that timely action can avert disaster. It is now that with foresight and will such action can be taken without disturbing the essence of our way of life, by adjusting behaviour not altering it entirely.

There is one further preliminary point. Just as science and technology has given us the evidence to measure the danger of climate change, so it can help us find safety from it. The potential for innovation and scientific discovery and hence, of course for business investment and growth, is enormous. With the right framework for action, the very art of solving it can unleash a new and benign commercial force to take the action forward, providing jobs, technology spin-offs and new business opportunities as well as protecting the world we live in.

Canadian scientists have brought this message home bluntly in a direct open letter to Prime Minister Stephen Harper, dated April 18, 2006:

As the climate changes, **there will be increasing impacts on Canada's natural ecosystems and on its socio-economic activities.** Some impacts are:

- Inadequate water for Prairie agriculture and hydroelectric utilities due to increased drying of the continental interior and reduced snow pack and shrinking glaciers;
- Threats to the sustainability of Canada's natural resources due to an inability of our ecosystems to respond rapidly as the climate changes.
  - Warming allowing the spread of insects through our forests and prolonged drought making forests more susceptible to fires;
- Warming of ocean and river waters, threatening survival of Pacific salmon, a cold water fish, by forcing it away from its spawning grounds;
- Increasing severity and frequency of some extreme weather events, including floods and droughts, some of which are already exceeding 100-year records and requiring more robust design specifications for infrastructure;
- Thawing of permafrost and associated effects on the human environment (infrastructure, roads, pipelines, buildings), sea ice, northern ecosystems and species, all leading to dramatic changes in the lives of northern people;
- Increased marine traffic through the northern sea routes, increasing the likelihood of environmental impacts and challenges to Canada's sovereignty claims in the Arctic.

Some of these projected impacts are already detectable.

The challenge is great, but it can be met. And in meeting it, we need to recognize that we can make our economy more innovative and create more jobs. The simplistic equation "jobs versus the environment" has to go. The future is about sustaining the economy, not weakening the creation of jobs and opportunity.

Prime Minister Jean Chrétien understood the dimensions of the problem when he signed the Kyoto Protocol on behalf of Canada. That decision needs to be followed by decisive action.

Stephen Harper's approach has been to deny the problem, and then to assert the banality that what is required is a "made in Canada" approach to a global problem.

There is something pathetic in denying the extent of the problem and pretending that all that is required is for Canada to join with other countries still in denial. The U.S. Senate voted 95-0 against joining Kyoto or anything like it. And yet, eleven years later, dozens of American cities are insisting that Kyoto's targets for emissions reduction have to be exceeded, and are taking steps to do just that. The direction of both scientific and policy thinking is heading down just one track, the steady reduction in greenhouse emissions by as much as 60 per cent by 2050.

Canadians don't want their country to be an environmental laggard. They are looking for leadership, knowing the future is in the balance. It is only leadership that will allow us to work with other countries, notably India and China, to come to terms with the effects of industrialization.

Global citizenship requires us to do more than just play along. Deeper strategies are essential to meet, and then surpass, targets for actually reducing greenhouses gases.

We have to ask why it is that in the face of an increasing weight of evidence, governments, businesses, institutions, and people downplay environmental risks and overplay social and economic benefits to continuing our current practices. Why is the cost of change consistently overplayed, and its benefits consistently underestimated?

Protecting the environment is not an emotion. It is not the soft option.

It is too easy to blame the other guy, to say that we don't make progress because of vested interests, the status quo, power structures, or short-term political expediency. We need a new forthrightness on this issue, a new kind of "risk-taking" that will be less risky in the long run. We need the courage to do the right thing. Canada needs to move beyond writing reports about corporate social responsibility and the "triple bottom line." This is the century where we will either come to terms with the environment or it will come to terms with us.

Reigning in resource consumption and cutting waste while growing our economy is critical to living more sustainably. So is thinking more systemically. The Earth's oceans, land, and atmosphere are systems. How we have produced energy for the past three hundred years has had a profound effect on each of these systems.

There is only one atmosphere. It surrounds the planet, absorbing ultraviolet solar radiation and regulating temperature extremes between day and night. Three-quarters of the atmosphere's mass is concentrated within eleven kilometres of the Earth's surface. And we are changing the very chemical makeup of this fragile atmosphere, affecting weather, climate, and the health of the environment and people through the global transport of pollution.

We live in a bubble. We need to give more thought to the protective membrane that makes up the air we breathe. We use the atmosphere like a landfill with no dumping fees charged: a free depository for pollution. It makes no sense. And this atmospheric landfill is filling up with toxic chemicals, heavy metals, ozone, acid gases, and greenhouse gases. Falling down as acid rain and bio-accumulating toxics that build up in the food chain; creating smog so thick that we can't see the horizon; thinning the ozone layer so more solar radiation gets through, burning plants and skin; and changing the energy balance driving our weather and climate system.

Our one atmosphere absorbs this chemical soup, carrying pollution from China into Japan, from the United States into Canada, from Asia into the Arctic. One atmosphere reacting to all these assaults, as it should: as a system. Acid rain, smog, ozone depletion, and climate change affect Earth and humanity each in their own way, and together as an interacting whole.

This is why debates on whether to tackle climate change or toxins and acid rain or smog, as if they are so easily divisible, are nonsensical. So is thinking we will get anywhere with "made in Canada" approaches that ignore the responsibility of collective international action. The absurdity of the debate becomes even more obvious when so many of the same sources of pollution cause the atmosphere so much trouble.

The upstream oil and gas sector, transportation, and electricity production are responsible for the majority of acid (sulphur dioxide and nitrogen oxide), carbon monoxide, and particulate emissions causing acid rain and smog and the greenhouse gases causing climate change. Industrial processes, particularly smelting, are critical sources of heavy metals and sulphur emissions.

We simply don't have the luxury of saying we will cut air pollution today and get to the climate change problem tomorrow. If the pollution causing acid rain and smog, for example, were to stop being emitted today because we installed "end of pipe" technologies, the atmosphere would cleanse itself of these irritants within weeks. If we stopped emitting greenhouse gas today, the Earth's climate would still continue to change. We have no choice. We must cut emissions of all pollutants, including greenhouse gases.

How much longer can we ignore the evidence? Since the 1950s, global damage from climate extremes has doubled every five to seven years, according to the insurance industry. Extreme climate events are resulting in fatalities, injuries, property damage, and severe economic dislocation. The increase in disaster losses is due to growth in the population and property located in regions of risk, aging public infrastructure, and increases in the frequency and severity of climate extremes. Hurricane Katrina cost the U.S. economy U.S.$100 billion, a figure far in excess of the projected cost of cutting greenhouse gas emissions to meet their Kyoto Protocol target. And that is just one storm.

The precautionary principle requires a response to the strengthening evidence in the scientific assessments of the Intergovernmental Panel on Climate Change (IPCC). The IPCC analysis shows that global average temperature increases above 2°C raises the risk of severe consequences for human health and security and the environment.

We must reduce greenhouse gas emissions and adapt to minimize the adverse impact of climate change that is now inevitable. Every segment of society, from major users and producers of energy to the smallest businesses and homeowners, can play a part. The federal government needs to work with its provincial/territorial and municipal partners to develop an energy framework for Canada that drives efficient resource consumption and low levels of waste.

Fortunately, opportunities abound. Globally, the International Energy Agency projects that $17 trillion in energy infrastructure spending is needed in the next twenty years to meet growing demands in developing countries and to replace aging infrastructure in developed countries.

In Canada, the Canadian Electricity Association says $150 billion in investment is needed in new supply and transmission infrastructure over the next twenty years, $7.5 billion a year, much of it in Ontario, Quebec, and Newfoundland and Labrador. In Alberta, the oil sands will see at least $40 billion of investment over the next six to ten years, increasing production from 1 million barrels a day to 5 million barrels a day. The federal government alone will contribute more than $16 billion by 2010 toward investments right across Canada in highways, transit, and municipal infrastructure that with bi-partite and tri-partite matching could easily exceed $50 billion. This is why I am advocating a federal "green infrastructure" fund, to help drive these needed investments using designs and technologies that contribute to sustainability.

Canada needs to play its part in the global energy revolution by ensuring that this more than $250 billion in investment positions Canada as a global leader and contributor to sustainable energy production and consumption. It needs to be a world energy leader, acting ethically to take responsibility for the environmental impact of its energy production and consumption by ensuring our citizens use energy efficiently and responsibly. And in doing the right thing, Canada will make its economy more competitive, innovative, and sustainable. An integrated solution to a systemic problem.

Responding to scientific concern, the global community agreed in 1992 to begin to take steps to resolve the climate problem by agreeing to the Framework Convention on Climate Change. The UN agreement included a voluntary commitment to stabilize greenhouse gas emissions at 1990 levels by the year 2000 and was ratified by more than 180 countries. Acknowledging that voluntary approaches were not influencing global emissions and with increasing scientific certainty about the causes and risks of climate change, the UN negotiated the Kyoto Protocol in 1997, setting for the first time legally binding quantified emission reduction obligations for developed countries. The total average reduction for developed and economy-in-transition countries was 5.2 per cent below 1990 levels by 2012, a small but significant step forward. Canada agreed to contribute to the total obligation by reducing its greenhouse gas emissions 6 per cent below 1990 levels by 2012. The Kyoto Protocol became international law when Russia ratified in 2004, setting the stage for "entry into force" February 16, 2005. More than 160 countries have ratified the Kyoto Protocol, including China, India, Brazil, and Mexico. The United States and Australia did not ratify the Protocol, eroding its emission reduction potential to about 3 per cent below 1990, but remain signatories to the Convention.

The Kyoto Protocol was the first modest step toward the deep and sustained reductions in greenhouse gases needed to slow climate change. Developed countries agreed to take the first step because their emissions since the Industrial Revolution were primarily responsible for the climate change we are seeing today. Developing countries were asked to commit to taking action to reduce emissions but were not asked to take on a legally binding emission reduction target. It was widely expected that countries with rapidly emerging economies like China, Brazil, Mexico, Singapore, and South Korea would take on increasingly stringent obligations in subsequent commitment periods.

The Kyoto Protocol also established critical infrastructure for reporting, monitoring, and emissions trading that are building the foundation for future, deeper reductions by all countries. Negotiations on what should happen post-2012 after the first commitment period ends were launched in Montreal in 2005 under the leadership of Canada with Stéphane Dion in the chair. As president of the Conference of the Parties, Canada was responsible for securing the Montreal Plan of Action, setting in motion the operating rules for the Protocol that only becomes operational in 2008 and the negotiating process for dealing with the next steps.

Canada appeared to cross a threshold, leading international discussions about next steps and acknowledging it must do more to get its contribution to the problem under control.

That momentum was lost on January 23, 2006, when a new minority Conservative government was elected and quickly announced Canada would not meet its Kyoto target. Canada is the first country in the world that has ratified the Kyoto Protocol to say it is dropping out, thus undermining the global effort. We have become an environmental deadbeat, looking for excuses instead of solutions.

This is an embarrassment for Canada. Parties to the Kyoto Protocol were to report on "demonstrable progress" toward their targets in January 2006. Of the twenty-six reporting countries, the United Kingdom and

Sweden have already met their targets. Finland and Greece will meet their targets with additional measures. Denmark, Japan, Switzerland, the Netherlands, Belgium, Norway, Spain, and the EU (EU15) are projected to meet their targets with additional domestic measures and the use of international mechanisms like the Clean Development Mechanism. All economies in transition countries have already met their targets.

Many of the same countries that are on track to meet their Kyoto Protocol targets are the same countries that rank high internationally on productivity and innovation. International experience is demonstrating that a "productivity agenda" and an "environmental sustainability" agenda *do* go together.

As I have discussed earlier, it is precisely this shift to an innovation and learning culture that will at once increase our prosperity and make our growth sustainable. In short, we need to:

- maximize Canada's comparative advantage;
- accelerate substitution in production processes;
- lead in the development of international and domestic carbon trading markets;
- reward innovation through stretch targets, performance-based regulation, and incentives;
- establish clusters for energy innovation and diversification
- invest in skills development; and
- rebrand Canada as a world supplier of leading-edge energy products and services.

Can Canada meet its international obligations under the Kyoto Protocol at this late date? It will be difficult. Should we abandon our commitment? Absolutely not. That would not be the ethical thing to do. Nor would it be the right thing for Canadian society or the economy.

The right thing to do is for Canada to take strong steps now that demonstrate to the world that we are serious about climate change and that we are taking control of our contribution to it. We need to build a foundation for long-term reductions. The big three in terms of priorities are electricity, transportation, and oil and gas production.

By way of illustration, here are some things we could do in each of these sectors:

1. Electricity: Greenhouse gas emissions from the electricity sector grew by 35 million tonnes between 1990 and 2004 as a result of growing demand and heavier reliance on coal. Now is the time to drive $150 billion of projected investment toward outcomes that emphasize low or zero-emitting electricity sources that also contribute to increasing resiliency and reliability of the electricity system. While investment in centralized large-scale supply and transmission is essential, so, too, is investment in distributed energy systems like wind, solar, and community energy systems that don't rely solely on centralized generation and transmission. Targeting these self-reliant systems as a priority in locations housing emergency facilities – police, fire, hospitals, water treatment and wastewater plants – and in

our homes, buildings, and institutions can make communities safe in the face of extreme events.

The government of Canada can set national objectives for renewable energy. Building on provincial and territorial targets for renewable energy and energy efficiency and conservation, the federal government can set and support through tax policy and incentives national stretch objectives for renewable energy and energy efficiency improvements through a clean energy framework. It can regulate emissions from fossil fuels used to generate electricity through the Canadian Environmental Protection Act and it can bring electricity producers into a nationally coordinated cap and trade allowance trading system that would include oil and gas producers and all large industrial emitters. We need to support pilot projects demonstrating power plant carbon capture and sequestration technologies.

2. Transportation: Emissions from road transportation rose by 36 per cent between 1990 and 2004 because people are driving farther, but also because the fleet-mix is changing as the number of light trucks on the road between 1990 and 2004 doubled. Emissions from heavy-duty vehicles rose between 1990 and 2004, an 83 per cent increase as a result of free trade, deregulation of the trucking industry, and demand for just-in-time delivery. Stringent federal efficiency and tailpipe standards for cars and trucks are essential. Canada must commit to tailpipe standards for greenhouse gases that would cut emissions 30 per cent between 2009 and 2016. A federal priority should be to ensure we work collaboratively with

Canadian manufacturers to build efficient and new technology vehicles right here at home for domestic and U.S. markets.

3. Oil and gas production: Between 1990 and 2004, greenhouse gas emissions from the upstream fossil fuel industry increased to 130 million tonnes from 83.3 million tonnes for an increase of 64.1 per cent. Emissions reflect the 65 per cent increase in total production of oil and gas in the period, most of which was exported to the United States. Growth in net oil and gas exports grew by 513 per cent (almost ten times the rate of growth of oil production), while net exports of natural gas increased 138 per cent (almost twice the rate of growth of natural gas production). Over the period, the sum total of net oil and gas energy exports increased by 192 per cent. Oil sands development makes Canada an international energy player with an opportunity to lead the world in investment in carbon capture and sequestration technologies. Carbon dioxide is being captured and injected into depleting oil fields today to enhance oil recovery. We need to expand that effort.

Doing the right thing by the atmosphere must happen at the same time we are doing the right thing by our water and land to protect the environment that sustains our economy, health, and quality of life. Getting there will stimulate a revolution in energy systems, resource productivity, and industrial processes. In the process, Canada can lead the world in development of innovative, sustainable, and responsible resource exploitation and use.

I have written mainly about climate change because it is the number-one environmental challenge of the planet. Conservation – the support of our system of national parks and protected areas, the wild places in Canada – also has a global dimension. Every nation has a responsibility to ensure that the share of the planet's biodiversity within its borders be protected and that the preservation of species and their habitat is made a priority.

Enjoyment of Canada's wild places is integral to the Canadian imagination. The federal government has a responsibility to ensure that Parks Canada and the Canadian Wildlife Service bodies are resourced adequately to ensure that such protection becomes a reality. Pressure to develop natural resources, such as in the Mackenzie Valley, should be accompanied by the Protected Areas Strategy that has been developed collaboratively with Aboriginal peoples and territorial and provincial governments.

I am convinced that the goals of sustainable development, conservation, and a brighter future for Aboriginal communities, with good jobs and a real stake in natural resource projects, can co-exist. It requires looking ahead, being innovative, listening to the younger generation, and staying committed.

Getting there on climate change, and conservation, requires a shift in mindset from "we can't!" to "why not?" My experience has been that the public will accept change, and business can accept clear rules, if we engage in a transparent dialogue on the costs and benefits of what has to be done. We are in the world, and as natural multilateralists are engaged in finding solutions with our fellow passengers on the globe. We are also a manufacturing and resource-based country, in a climate that still knows cold. But the costs of doing nothing, or far too little, are much too high.

———⟫•⟪———

Making the Federal Idea Work for Canadians

WHAT IS THE ROLE OF THE FEDERAL GOVERNMENT today? Canadians want and expect governance that is open, transparent, accountable, and democratic. They are entitled to nothing less. Critical to this is a public service that is unequivocally committed to good governance. From my personal knowledge, that is the case – I grew up in a family where the great public servants of the day were mentors, friends, and, in a sense, heroes. My experience in government was that, in the vast majority, the public service was deeply committed to giving impartial advice and to accepting that governments were going to chart their own course. The best advice is not always followed.

I am not one of those who believes that "government is the problem." That is not to say that more spending and higher taxes are the answer to all our challenges. But it is to say that in modern society the provision of good services, effective and efficient regulation in the interests of public safety and public health, the protection of Canadians' security, and the promotion of Canada's interest internationally all require a thoughtful, active, and efficient government.

Let's start with some history. Canada has a federal structure because it was the only form of government that could allow us to stay together without stifling differences or having those differences drive us apart. The debates between 1840 and 1867 are very instructive. The political community of the day concluded that the "Durham model" of a single central government for Ontario and Quebec couldn't work. It cramped both English and French. It led to political paralysis.

Hence the BNA Act. The document itself is quite centralist in its bias – this certainly reflected Sir John A. Macdonald's own views, as he set out in his famous letter to M.C. Cameron:

> My dear Cameron . . . As to things political I must try to discuss the federation scheme with you. I'm satisfied that we've hit upon the only practical plan. I do not mean to say the best plan. . . . We've avoided exciting local prejudice against the scheme by protecting local interests and, at the same time, have raised a strong central government. If the confederation goes on you,

if spared the ordinary age of man, will see both local parliaments and governments absorbed in the general power. This is as plain to me as if I saw it accomplished now. Of course, it does not do to adopt that point of view in discussing this subject in lower Canada.

So it was that in the 1867 model, the Senate would not be elected but would be appointed by the prime minister. Federally appointed lieutenant-governors would be able to turn back legislation, and wayward provincial legislators could have their laws disallowed by the federal Parliament.

It was the Privy Council in London, early in the last century, that interpreted the Constitution in such a way that the provinces' equality as partners in the federation was made unequivocal. Macdonald's vision of the "central power" taking over everything evaporated into the ether. Labour relations, a critical issue in the industrializing country of the early twentieth century, became an area of provincial jurisdiction. The ownership of natural resources by the provinces put "province-building" on a par with nation-building. While both World Wars gave temporary centralizing powers to the federal government, these did not last forever.

The issue of our time is not how to retreat to a world of firewalls, silos, and watertight compartments. Rather, the central issue is how do we get governments to work more effectively together on issues that matter to Canadians. Health care, child care, life-long learning, emissions reductions, securities commissions, mobility: these are words and concepts not found in the 1867 Constitution. So returning to that pristine and austere world is not possible, even if it were desirable.

I mention the origin because sometimes people talk about "getting back to the basics of 1867." This does not get us anywhere. Canada then was a largely rural, agricultural country. It is now predominantly urban. The kind of centralism envisaged by Macdonald in relation to "local governments" is clearly impossible.

In my own work around the world, I have concluded that the value of autonomy is closely linked to several distinct trends: political, cultural, economic, and technological. The political and cultural trend is most often manifested in the persistence of the bonds of language and local identity. Were Karl Marx and John Stuart Mill to come back to life and meet for a conversation in a Highgate coffee house, they would each have to admit that the world has not evolved as they had predicted and hoped. They both believed that ethnic nationalism was a phenomenon whose force would diminish in the face of technology and enlightenment. Their "end game" was quite different – but both nineteenth-century liberalism and Marxism shared the view that religious belief and linguistic identity would ultimately cede to scientific rationality.

Things have worked out differently, as we have learned at great expense. Identity – of language, race, religion – has proven remarkably persistent. The demand for self-government, at the political level, is closely linked to this persistence. Nationalism has not gone away. Nor have local identity and a sense of geographic community.

These trends are reinforced by the forces of the marketplace. The command economies have, for the most part, collapsed. Central planning has been forced to give way to more flexible and decentralized forms of economic management. Cities have become critical engines of growth. All governments have had to replace the skills of rowing with those of steering, to borrow a well-known phrase. This is what is behind the broad trend to devolution throughout the world.

Understanding the role of new technologies in this transformation is key. The forms of governance that respond to the Digital Revolution will be different from those that responded to the Industrial Revolution. They will, at once, be more global and more local. The emergence of "city states" in this new economy is no accident. Nor is their demand for more autonomy.

The highly centralized nation-state then faces challenges from within, as well as outside. Local and regional governments want more autonomy and more resources to do their job. The quality of local infrastructure will have much to do with success in the global economy. At the same time, the governance of these globalizing forces requires an international perspective.

The federal conversation is the critical dialogue of the twenty-first century. Federalism has emerged in countries that are escaping the old world of centralist ideologies and hierarchical thinking. It puts the drive to autonomy in context; freedom is balanced with responsibility.

There has been a profound resurgence in interest in the federal idea in the last decade. I choose the phrase *federal idea* carefully because the "ism" in federalism has a way of limiting debate and understanding. In Spain, the central government is reluctant to use the word because it seems to connote the dissolution of sovereign authority; conversely, the Catalonians won't use it because in their eyes it does not sufficiently represent the unique nature of the Catalan claim to self-government. In South Africa, the word fell into disrepute because it had some official approval from the apartheid government; similarly, the African National Congress's vision of "one South Africa" made the party reluctant to describe any new constitution as "federalist."

These are hardly new debates: the Jeffersonian tradition in American politics was proud to call itself "anti-federalist" because it concluded that the centralizing forces behind John Adams and Alexander Hamilton had branded the "f-word." Yet both Thomas Jefferson and John Adams were clearly federalists who shared far more key assumptions than the rhetoric of democratic debate might have led some to believe.

What is happening today in South Africa, Spain, Mexico, Nigeria, the United Kingdom, Russia, Brazil, India, Pakistan, Cyprus, India, Iraq, and Sri Lanka, to mention just a few countries, is a reflection of some important common tendencies that need to be understood. There is certainly more than one way to be a federalist; it is the common idea that matters.

Political arrangements of co-operation and association have their roots in many ancient societies, from

African tribal councils to city-state pacts to the Iroquois Confederacy. The modern federal idea is first and foremost a democratic idea. It implies a respect for people's identities and their political choices. It is incompatible with populist concepts of democracy that are not based on a respect for individual rights, constitutional process, and the rule of law. It also runs against those elements in society who believe they have a pipeline to the "real" or "best" interests of the people. Ideologies that express a certain knowledge of political truth (or religious truths as made manifest in the world) are implacable enemies of the federal idea.

The federal idea, therefore, understands the vitality of politics and rival notions of the public interest. It also speaks to a common concern about limiting the sphere of government. Constitutions that set out which level of government can do what, and then also guarantee rights and freedoms, if they are combined with a court structure with the capacity to interpret this balance – and to enforce that interpretation – are inevitably about the limits of popular sovereignty and the protection of both group and individual rights.

These points are basic to the defining element of the federal idea, namely that a federal country is one where power is at once divided and coordinated. That, of course, is the central tension in federalism: it is not just "one idea." It implies a common agreement to do certain things separately and other things together. It is about more than just devolution, because the premise is that state or provincial governments have as much sovereignty in their sphere as the national or federal government have in theirs. There are no "higher" or "lower" governments, no "senior" or "junior" governments, just different governments doing different things within a common framework. Nor is the national government a mere creature of the provinces, delegated by them to do certain tasks. It, too, has its own sovereignty, its own direct connection to the people.

The federal idea, therefore, implies an ongoing, indeed a never-ending, dialogue about who does what. There are significant issues in each federation about fiscal issues, how money is raised, how it is shared, how it is spent. In Canada, resources are provincially owned and the direct revenue from that flows to different provincial governments. In Nigeria, the central government claims all oil revenue and then divides it up according to a formula. With the return of democratic federalism to that country, the issue of how revenue should be divided is now being argued in courts of law and the courts of public opinion. Australia's revenue-sharing formula is said to be so complicated that it brings to mind the British statesman's comment that "there are only three people who know the causes of the Crimean War. Two of them are dead and I can't remember."

There is a growing consensus that local and state governments need to be able to raise the money to spend on their own programs: this increases both transparency and accountability. Where this is not possible, central-revenue sharing needs to be both more clear and less unilateral. When this doesn't happen, as is often the case, it gives rise to inevitable conflict.

Those opposed to federalism point to these conflicts and the alleged cost of too many governments as justification either for simply abolishing regional governments altogether or for separatism. Federalism has often been opposed by elements of the majority because it is said to imply costs in countries that are "too small" for federal arrangements. One also hears arguments from determined minorities that the right of self-determination is absolute, and that federalism adds too much complexity to the simplicity of separate states.

We should be skeptical of these claims. They have little basis in fact. It would be hard to point to the "efficiency" of a one-party Mexico or the Nigeria of the military dictatorships. Switzerland is geographically small and politically complex. Yet it has remained for decades a symbol of effective governance.

The federal idea is indeed about the complexity of things, but better the give-and-take of an endless negotiation – isn't that what much of life itself is, anyway? – than the simple desert of the Jacobin, the Leninist, the militarist, the religious fanatic, or even the old-fashioned ethnic nationalist whose world has difficulty with any kind of pluralism.

The resurgence of the federal idea has at its core many different causes. The vitality of the values of democracy, the revolutions in the politics of identity and human rights, the twin collapse of apartheid and bureaucratic communism, the impact of the technological revolution, the economic changes we associate with the word *globalization*: all these have made their contribution. In Mexico, for example, one-party rule for most of the twentieth century meant that while the constitution spoke of the federal nature of the country, the reality was quite different. The same was even truer for the Soviet Union. The man on horseback had an equally brutal effect in Brazil and Nigeria: the federal idea is quite incompatible with the command and control mentality of the military hierarchy.

This renewal is not at all confined to countries that have a federalist tradition. Countries have long had to struggle with the simple truth that geography is rarely synonymous with automatic homogeneity.

The federal idea is part of another trend as well. European co-operation since the 1950s has now led to an elected European parliament common court, freedom of movement as well as free trade, and a common currency. Supranational federalism is now a reality, despite extensive mutterings. National sovereignty is not dead, and the nation-state is not over. But the notion that these are exclusive or all defining is clearly outmoded. Governance practices within countries are inevitably subject to the scrutiny of world political and economic opinion and, most important, to the rule of law itself.

At the conclusion of the Mont Tremblant Conference on federalism in 1999, President Bill Clinton remarked that "maybe the federal idea isn't such a bad idea after all." He was right. The collapse of one-party states, the demands of identity, the urge to local empowerment, the insistence on greater openness and transparency in government, and the recognition that in a smaller and much more interdependent world "sovereignty" is no longer an absolute has brought the federal idea to the fore again.

Canadians should be proud of what we have accom- plished. No country is perfect, and institutions can always be improved. But we have to be careful not to embrace the rhetoric of those who suggest there is a fundamental flaw in the Canadian idea.

There is an almost catechismic quality to the question, Do you believe in the fiscal imbalance? The fiscal success of the federal government in eliminating budgetary deficits and, since 1998, actually starting to pay down the national debt is a positive achievement for Canada. When unemployment and inflation are both down, and revenues are healthy, this is precisely the wise and prudent moment to be reducing debt, just as in our own lives it makes sense to pay off the mortgage when you can.

The resentment of the provinces stems from the needs they have to fund: health-care costs are rising in excess of inflation; they have to deal with the challenge of giving enough to education, which is a priority; plus the infrastructure costs of cities. The severity of cuts in transfers from Ottawa that took place at earlier times needs to be fully understood and addressed.

To the fiscal imbalance question has now been added a renewed debate about equalization. Each province and region has its own unique perspective. The Council of the Federation has a report. So does the federal government. The formulas are complex.

There is no magic bullet that will resolve these issues for all time. The provinces and the federal government have been arguing about money and jurisdiction since

1867. But that does not mean the issues are hopeless.

I make these suggestions. The first is to remember that equalization is a constitutional principle, not a political indulgence. When premiers argue about formulas they are arguing about money, not the principle. An eventual compromise will have to be reached. Equalization is a federal responsibility. Its calculation should be based on an all-province assessment of wealth and fiscal capacity, and obviously be tempered by a realistic assessment of what is financially possible for the federal treasury. But the principle is clear: the access of Canadians to good education and health should not depend on accidents of birth and geography. Being a Canadian citizen should have real meaning.

The federal government can also help ease a financial burden on the provinces by uploading, rather than simply downloading. If the federal government were to take over provincial catastrophic drug plans (or at least those that wanted to do so) and take full responsibility for that part of the health-care system, this would mean greater efficiency, greater buying power, and an alignment of the federal drug approval power with the federal government plan.

Third, there should be a real effort to simplify the tax system, and to establish a much clearer connection in the public mind between particular taxes and the programs they are paying for. Right now, cities are confined to some user fees and licences, property taxes, a negotiated share of the federal gas tax, and the begging bowl. This is wrong. Both the provinces and the federal government are taxing consumption (sales tax and GST), income, liquor, gasoline, and on and on. There is a more creative, efficient way to do all of this.

If we are going to create an environmentally sustainable economy, there is no getting around paying for the real costs and impacts of energy, water use, and roads. The issue is to make sure we use the income tax system more creatively, giving more assistance and relief to middle- and low-income tax payers. While it is true that consumption taxes, tolls, and user fees are not progressive, they can have the advantage of linking payment to service and can encourage less consumption. Their impact on low-income Canadians can be offset by a more progressive approach to income taxes.

There are other key areas of federal-provincial co-operation: early childhood education; post-secondary education and training; environmental regulation; Aboriginal issues; and on it goes. Modern life is all about where jurisdictions meet, not in pretending that there are eternal boundaries between them.

The post-secondary education federal role supporting research, innovation, and graduate study needs to be strengthened, as do transfers to all provinces for the operating needs of colleges and universities. The focus of student assistance should be on living and tuition costs for all students attending training or post-secondary programs. Everyone wanting to study or train should be able to do so without fear of excessive debt.

The first job of the federal government is to help keep the country together. I was a supporter of patriation, Meech, Charlottetown, and the Clarity Act. I knocked on doors and campaigned in the referendums of 1980, 1992, and 1995. To break up Canada would be unforgivable. The notion that there would be "no cost" and only "net benefit" to Quebec and Quebecers is a terrible illusion. The distinctiveness of Quebec is not just about a legal and constitutional formula. It is a fact of life, recognized in 1867, and accepted as a reality of our Canadian existence.

Canadians want both prosperity and justice. Their government at all levels should be focused on the same thing and what they should do together to help achieve it. While the constitutional odyssey is never over, we should not get diverted into a morass of theories and formulas. Rather, we should be finding practical ways to solve problems.

If Quebec's place within the federation is a subject that has dominated political discussion in Canada, the issue of Aboriginal self-government is no less important. Canada's First Nations people faced disease, assimilation, and violent confrontation as they encountered European settlement. While the British negotiated treaties that recognized historic rights, these treaties did not receive recognition in 1867 beyond the assigning of responsibility for "Indian affairs" to the federal government.

It was a common nineteenth-century assumption that the Aboriginal population of Canada would eventually either die out or become completely assimilated. Fortunately, neither happened. Since the 1960s, Canada has seen a steady growth in its Aboriginal population and a strong reassertion of collective rights. These claims have had, since the Nisga'a case of the 1970s, the consistent support of the Supreme Court of Canada, which has reminded Canadians of our responsibility to recognize historic treaty obligations. These rights and obligations have not been adequately spelled out in the Constitution, but they were explicitly referred to in the entrenched Charter and were widely discussed in the debates over the Charlottetown Accord.

It now seems well established in Canadian law that treaties will be interpreted in a liberal and generous manner, and will in turn lead to discussions between band councils and governments on the principle of self-government. The agreement with the Nisga'a tribe off the B.C. coast is extensive and complex; it is clearly an example of a "third level of government," whose autonomy is significant. Similar agreements over land, mineral and resource management, education, and social services, as well as revenue sharing, have been and are being discussed and negotiated across the country.

The division of the Northwest Territories into two separate, self-governing entities, including Nunavut, where the Inuit people are in a clear majority, is also reflective of a significant devolution of powers to governments that do not have the full capacity of a province but are still governing in important respects. This will remain a key issue in the future, as the territories seek more autonomy and financial independence. Liberals will need to be responsive to these claims.

When I was premier of Ontario, I took steps to address Aboriginal issues on a nation-to-nation basis. This was not widely accepted in Canada at the time, and the Liberal government of Jean Chrétien had not yet launched the important policy of self-government. My approach, and the later policy of the federal Liberal government, acknowledged the importance of Aboriginal communities running their own affairs in their own communities. Dealing on this nation-to-nation basis helped create a climate of trust, and allowed us to make headway on issues of health, education, and economic development.

The place of First Nations, Inuit, and Métis in Confederation is constitutionally recognized under section 35 of our Charter of Rights and Freedoms. Since the Charter, the interpretations of the courts have contributed to righting many decades of wrongs. There is no turning back the page. Governments who think this is possible risk exhausting the goodwill that has begun and wasting opportunity for all Canadians.

The reality is that the living conditions in many Aboriginal communities today are at the level of developing countries. Health status, educational levels, access to jobs remain far below the levels in the non-Aboriginal population. This is simply not acceptable in a country as well off as ours. The attitudes that have fed these failures were wrong and quite incongruous with Canadian attitudes of accommodation, respect, tolerance, and anti-colonialism in other spheres.

Recognizing interdependence, dealing nation to nation, acknowledging Aboriginal and treaty rights, respecting inherent rights of self-government, committing to sharing equitably in the resources located on and near traditional territories: these are the foundations of success. Any efforts to secure healing and reconciliation, close the health gap, and pursue economic and educational opportunity and community development are situated within these principles.

Aboriginal peoples need greater control over decisions if they are to succeed in improving their quality of life. It cannot be achieved through "imposed" polices, as was tried in the past. Recognition of jurisdiction over health, housing, education – these are key. The pre-condition for success lies in finding solutions *with*, not *for*, Aboriginal Canadians.

And in stressing that rights and obligations must be respected, it is important to acknowledge that the Métis have also made a distinctive contribution to the country's development and shared history. The Métis are also a people with rights, a unique culture, and it is the obligation of governments in Canada to respect this. For too long Métis rights and culture were also not respected, with governments tending to lump their needs in with broader policies for Aboriginal peoples.

We should insist that the current federal government support the historic Canada-Métis Nation Framework Agreement between the Métis Nation and the federal government, signed in May 2005. This accord will strengthen the relationship between Canada and the Métis, and help establish a mutually acceptable negotiation process for Métis rights.

As a distinct Aboriginal nation, Métis-specific programs should be supported by the federal government. These programs need to evolve out of a collective process and, again, not simply be imposed. We must work collaboratively to help ensure that improved health, education, and better economic opportunities for Métis also become a reality.

Inuit and Aboriginal communities "north of 60" also have rights that must be respected, and land claim and other agreements must be arrived at soon, particularly as more natural resource opportunities emerge in Canada's North, of which Aboriginal peoples should receive a fair share.

The rights agenda and the development agenda are interdependent.

The historic Kelowna Accord represents the foundation for this new and better departure. Kelowna is not just a word. It was a remarkable process that saw thirteen provincial and territorial premiers and a prime minister working with the five major Aboriginal organizations over fourteen months to achieve consensus on a way forward to close the gap between Aboriginal and non-Aboriginal standards of living and opportunities.

There was clearly conviction on the part of all parties to achieve a workable end result. And they got there. It was a pledge by the Crown to Aboriginal peoples. That is why it is simply unacceptable for the Harper government to somehow claim that "it was not signed," or that "it was written on the back of an envelope," or that "the money was never booked." These are disingenuous dodges by the government of Canada, and Harper should be called out on them.

With half the population in Aboriginal communities under the age of twenty-five, they are by far the fastest-growing demographic in Canada. More, not less, investment is required, and we need to move quickly to ensure this generation ends up better, not worse off than their parents. We need this younger generation to be active contributors to our national well-being, and to fill the job market that will be vacated as the boomer generation nears retirement.

Out of the Kelowna Accord, we need to address four broad themes: treaty obligations; economic opportunity; social and living conditions; and transparency and accountability.

Treaty obligations with Aboriginal peoples must be respected in both spirit and intent. This means putting adequate resources into expediting existing land-claim and self-government processes and properly funding the implementation aspects of those agreements.

Economic opportunity is key to being masters in one's own house. Aboriginal governments must have the capacity to raise the revenues they require for the members of their communities.

The natural-resource sector holds out the greatest potential at the present time for good job opportunities for these communities. Canada's resource sector is, at the same time, dependent on long-term certainty of access to land and skilled labour. In many cases, oil, gas, diamond, and other resources are on or adjacent to, or dependent on access across, Aboriginal lands. This is another reason why conclusion of negotiations over outstanding land claims is so important to the Canadian economy. Aboriginal communities can be a source of the labour supply needed to realize the potential of these resource opportunities.

Non-Aboriginal parts of society have benefited disproportionately from extraction of these resources in the past. That, too, must become a thing of the past. Aboriginal people deserve to share fully in the benefits that flow from resource development, particularly through employment, contracting opportunities, and equity ownership. Resource revenue-sharing is an issue whose time has come and must be addressed.

The Mackenzie Valley pipeline initiative represents a golden opportunity to get it right and meet Canada's needs for cleaner energy, resource revenue-sharing, training, and job opportunities for Inuit and First Nations.

Internet access will also play a key role in expanding horizons and opportunities, and running a modern business or the affairs of a government. Business, health, education, preservation and dissemination of culture, and communication with other Aboriginal communities facing similar issues can all be facilitated by broadband access. The federal government has an obligation to ensure that the "digital divide" is addressed with respect to First Nations and that Internet access is provided as soon as possible to remote communities.

Social and living conditions in Aboriginal communities remain far below national averages. These gaps are an

embarrassment to a nation such as ours. Health, education, infrastructure, and housing need a major push and
the kind of innovative approaches that emerged from the
Kelowna process, including the Canada-Aboriginal
Peoples Roundtable. Telehealth should be available to
Aboriginal communities. Grants, bursaries, and scholarships should be sufficient to ensure that no qualified
Aboriginal student is denied the opportunity for post-
secondary education.

Access to clean water on reserves must be addressed
as swiftly as possible. To that end, training, infrastructure
needs, and such innovations as assistance through remote
monitoring of water quality need to be explored.

Finally, close to half our Aboriginal population now
lives in urban areas. The federal government needs to
take a leadership role in bringing provinces, Aboriginal
groups, and service-providers together to work through
how we address the challenges facing Canada's urban
aboriginal constituency.

Accountability and transparency must guide us
in all that we undertake with the Aboriginal peoples of
Canada. And it must be recognized that "accountability"
is not a one-way street. The government of Canada
needs to be held to account for public reporting on outcomes, including poor outcomes, and held to account as
well for expediting negotiations on outstanding claims.
Leaders in First Nations communities in turn need to be
accountable and transparent to their communities. Much
of this still needs to be worked out, but in this era, it is
an aspect of the agenda that cannot be neglected.

Canada's North, the Yukon, the Northwest Territories, and Nunavut are regions of unparalleled natural beauty, distinct challenges, and great opportunity. The voice and perspectives of the three unique territories with their diverse populations – including First Nations, Métis, and Inuit peoples – and the opportunity associated with an abundance of resource wealth including oil, gas, and diamonds need to be championed within the federation.

We can put real commitment behind the words "a Canada from sea to sea to sea." Resource development and the potential of major pipeline construction are bringing and will continue to bring immense benefits to southern Canadians. But if we are to realize the great promise of the North, we can't ignore the need to address land claims, revenue sharing, education and training, and, of course, climate change.

An economically strong North with self-reliant, healthy, and educated populations will be central to the nation's prosperity in coming years, helping to provide secure continental energy supplies. It will require innovative solutions to such challenges as creating unique and workable governance and sharing arrangements between Aboriginal and non-Aboriginal communities, building a national transportation infrastructure that serves all regions, limiting the effects of global warming, as well as contributing to the Nation's Arctic sovereignty and security.

A Northern agenda and an Aboriginal peoples' agenda are linked. Maturity, generosity, a sense of the past, hope for the future, a will to find solutions, a relationship built on respect and equality, adequate funding, and control over one's destiny and affairs are the ingredients that will lead to success for the Aboriginal peoples of Canada. They are the principles and the ingredients to which I remain firmly committed.

Finally, we have to be more aware of an emerging issue: the autonomous powers of municipalities. Canada's structure in the nineteenth century was largely rural. We now have urban agglomerations of millions of people. They still have the legal status of "provincial creatures," and this increasingly rubs against the contemporary grain. Provincial and federal authorities invest too little in cities. The cities demand more power, more ability to govern themselves, and, most important, the ability to raise money. The federal government and the provinces are under pressure to yield in all three areas, which they will ultimately have to do.

Writing more than a century ago, the French sociologist Ernest Renan posed the question, What is a nation? He pointed out that religion, race, ethnicity, and language could not be seen as the defining core of a country. They were each too restrictive and confining, too exclusive of the competing realities within any political community. He came to the simple conclusion that a nation was simply a group of people who had chosen to do great things together in the past and who choose to do them together in the future.

This has the advantage of assuring mutual tolerance, civic peace, and a political identity that transcends race and religion. Our best political leaders have always understood this. Our worst ones have chosen to ignore it, and have consistently led us to dead ends.

The federal government needs to be open to change, to the demands that will inevitably come from provinces, from First Nations, from municipalities. But in being responsive, the Canadian government cannot lose sight of its own responsibilities. There is nothing to be gained if the national government loses its way, its sense of where we need to go as citizens. Our federalism is not a recipe for a retreat to a tiny, diminishing role: an enduring partnership like Canada still needs the fibre of leadership.

Canada in the World

SPEAKING IN OSLO, NORWAY, ON DECEMBER 11, 1957, Lester B. Pearson said when receiving the Nobel Prize, "The choice... is as clear now for nations as it was once for the individual: peace or extinction. The life of states cannot, any more than the life of individuals, be conditioned by the force and will of a unit, however powerful, but by the consensus of a group, which must one day include all states."

Pearson then described what he called his "four faces of peace": peace and prosperity, peace and power, peace and diplomacy, and peace and people. He spoke eloquently of the need for a focus on open trade, collective security, and a commitment to a spirit of open dialogue and increased trade between states and the peoples of the world.

Pearson quoted the great judge Learned Hand: "Most of the issues that mankind sets out to settle, it never does settle ... [the dispute] disappears because it is replaced by some compromise that, although not wholly acceptable to either side, offers a tolerable substitute for victory."

To Pearson's four faces of peace we should add one more: peace and the sustainability of the planet. Above all, we should speak to the world with a spirit of engagement and commitment, as Lester Pearson did.

Our foreign policy should reflect both our interests and our values. The debate as to whether what we do in the world should be realistic or idealistic is pretty empty. It should be both.

We are just over 30 million people, an advanced economy with sovereignty over vast lands on the northern half of the North American economy. Well over half our national income depends on trade outside our borders, most of it with the United States.

We are an Aboriginal country as well as a country of immigrants and settlers. The Inuit people of the Far North want a deep connection with other peoples in other polar communities. Our sensitivity and understanding of issues of climate change, cultural and educational challenge, and resource development will inevitably reflect this part of the Canadian reality.

The Aboriginal/settler dynamic will also be reflected in how we connect with countries and communities with similar issues. From Australia to Mexico to Russia, questions of human rights, economic and community development, and cultural integrity are part of a shared experience. We need to embrace this part of our personality and recognize it as part of our international policy.

So, too, with Quebec. Its preoccupation with issues of culture, language, and education naturally lead to a concern about Quebec's identity having an international voice. This is entirely appropriate, and threatens no one. Canada will benefit from a Quebec presence on its delegation to UNESCO. Canada will speak with one voice on security and defence issues. But the range of that voice will be all the richer because of our diversity.

We are a country deeply committed to the rule of law, to human rights, to the value of an open society, to democracy, to federalism, to equality, to a deep sense of what we owe one another as citizens. We are proud of our values, what we have as a country. We have no imperial ambitions, nor should we see ourselves as anyone else's foot soldiers in imperial adventures. We have learned the hard way that the resolution of disputes and conflicts is difficult and requires extraordinary persistence.

When Canada became a federal country in 1867, our foreign policy was run by the British. Border disputes with the Americans, arguments about trade, and our foreign obligations were all handled for us. The federal Cabinet that declared war in 1914 was presided over by the Governor General, Prince Arthur, the Duke of Connaught and Strathearn. But as young Canadian boys died in the thousands on the battlefields of northern France, our identity came to the fore. Our identity owes much to Vimy Ridge.

Canada joined the League of Nations in 1919. We shared the hardships of the Great Depression in the 1930s and like many others were fooled for a time into thinking that reason would work its charm on Hitler. We fought on the battlefields again and assumed our place at the United Nations in the years after the Second World War. We were a founder of NATO. A Canadian, John Humphrey, drafted the UN Declaration of Human Rights. We are natural internationalists, we value multilateral institutions. That is who we are.

We are a trading nation, whose interests are best served by strong multilateral agreements and the rule of law. We can't just swing our weight around – nor can we rely on others' kindness. We depend on the wide range of agreements and instruments that connect us so strongly to the rest of the world.

It was the Liberal Party that negotiated Canada's entry into the General Agreement on Tariffs and Trade (GATT) and the Tories who thought Canada could somehow get preferred and guaranteed access to the U.S. market with the Free Trade Agreement.

Stephen Harper described the recent draft settlement on softwood as a "win-win." It was certainly a win for the United States. It was a loss for Canada: after decades of struggle, Canada left a full billion dollars on the table, abandoned its legal case, committed industry to restricting exports, and agreed to pay an additional tariff in the event lumber falls below $350 per thousand board feet. Some win.

This guarantees very tough times for the industry. It

also confirms that the U.S. Senate, where less than 20 per cent of the population control more than half the seats, will be a central hotbed of protectionism for American natural resources and agriculture.

NAFTA was sold to Canadians on the basis that free trade would be guaranteed by a binding dispute settlement. What the softwood deal clearly shows is that this simply isn't true. Canada consistently won its case before the binational panels. The U.S. industry got its way, with the support of the Senate and the administration.

Harper's Tories decided they would rather force the industry to surrender than support them in a tough battle with a powerful competitor.

What, then, of the future? The late John Kenneth Galbraith was surely right when he wrote in his 1996 book *The Good Society*:

> The move to a closer association between the peoples and institutions of the advanced countries cannot be resisted. It is on the great current of history; the social forces involved are beyond the influence of national legislatures, parliaments and politicians. The oratory may oppose it; the tide still will run. Nor should one wish otherwise.

This is certainly true when it comes to development – we need to bring punishing duties to an end for exports from Third World countries. We have to end protectionism against countries that want to trade their way to prosperity.

As Professor Jeffrey Sachs, the director of Columbia University's Earth Institute, wrote in his recent book, *The End of Poverty*:

> The antiglobalization movement leaders have the right moral fervor and ethical viewpoint, but the wrong diagnosis of the deeper problems ... too many protesters do not know that it is possible to combine faith in the power of trade and markets with understanding of their limitations as well. The movement is too pessimistic about the possibilities of capitalism with a human face, in which the remarkable power of trade and investment can be harnessed while acknowledging and addressing limitations through compensatory collective actions.

But this does not mean that Canada should abandon its agriculture and natural resource sectors to a theory. We should be smart traders as well as free traders. If the United States and Europe persist in extraordinary acts of subsidy to protect their farmers, we can hardly do less.

Does this make us inconsistent? Perhaps, but only to the extent that we are faced with the realities of deep inconsistency on the part of our neighbours. Freer trade will always be an important goal of public policy, but it won't work if we lower our guard while others keep theirs well defended.

The trade agenda can't be separated from the cause of international development. Nearly forty years ago, the World Bank asked Lester Pearson, then recently retired

as prime minister, to chair a study on development
assistance. One conclusion Pearson reached was that the
wealthier countries of the world should set aside 0.7
per cent of GDP to development assistance. In 2004–05,
Canada spent under half that amount on foreign assistance: $3.74 billion out of a federal budget of $224 billion.

Recently many countries have committed themselves
to meeting the "Pearson target." Denmark has already
reached the Pearson target, and is committed to staying
the course.

The point is not simply to meet a target or a number
for its own sake. I see the problem a different way. If thousands of children a day are dying in countries that are in
the clutches of extreme poverty, how can we help bring
this to an end?

These deaths attract no daily media coverage. They
have different causes: some by famine, disease, poverty,
conflict, and violence. But they are real and tragic enough.
We have trouble absorbing it. But we must respond, and
it will take concerted action.

Canada's GDP is currently $1.1 trillion, 0.7 per cent
of that is just $8 billion. We are currently spending less
than half that number on foreign assistance. So the math
of reaching the Pearson target is clear enough. Is it
doable in nine years? This naturally depends on priorities. It certainly can't be squared with the Conservative
math of a much smaller federal budget and GST cuts as
far as the eye can see. The trouble with the Tory vision is
that it is based on an attack on something they simply call
"government." It smears the public good by pretending

that taxes don't go to health care, education, and ending starvation abroad, but rather goes to something they call "bureaucracy" and "big government."

The poverty trap will only be ended over the next twenty years with increased spending on foreign assistance by countries like Canada. Canadians want their government to play a leadership role with an increased commitment.

We could lead the way by dramatizing the loss of life that is currently taking place and by celebrating any successes we can achieve in actually reducing it. What is remarkable is that so many Canadians are ahead of their government: it is impossible to travel the world without meeting volunteers, aid workers, teachers, and doctors from every corner of the country, leading the way, asking many times, Where is their government, why isn't it in the lead? The real Pearsonians are not only in Ottawa, but they are also working in AIDS orphanages in East Africa, removing land mines in Sri Lanka, teaching kids in northeast India, working on environmental issues in Costa Rica.

How, then, to respond to the threat of violence in the shrinking world? It is worth remembering that the twentieth century was the most violent and destructive in recorded history. Well-meaning people of the nineteenth century would have thought, and not just hoped, that the spread of education and a spirit of constant improvement would lead to a world of free trade and prosperity in which irrational war would have no place.

This isn't what happened. The clash of empires and nationalist ambition in the First World War led to the world's, and Canada's, first encounter with military conflict on a scale and level previously unimagined.

A victors' peace in 1919, a failed effort at collective security, and a global depression were the dry grass that allowed absolutist ideologies to catch fire and produce an even more violent, and global, conflict in the Second World War. Canadians in the tens of thousands lost their lives in these wars. We witnessed the Holocaust, a hugely destructive war in Asia and Europe, and a loss of life and hope that can hardly be imagined.

For nearly fifty years after the Second World War, it was the balance of terror of the Cold War that kept mass destruction at bay, but conflict of a different kind still erupted in Korea, the Middle East, and Vietnam. With the collapse of the Berlin Wall in 1989, it was first thought that a peace dividend would be paid and that military expenditure could be reduced dramatically in the East and West.

This is hardly the world in which we now find ourselves. Nor will it likely be a feature of the world of the next quarter-century. The insecurity and violence the world is now experiencing owes its origin to many diverse causes. Poverty and the destruction of the environment create a fierce struggle for resources, in which ideologies of faith and tribe can readily lead to armed conflict. An international arms industry creates a supply of weapons constantly available to both regimes and guerilla groups. Religious fundamentalism provides simplistic and profoundly dangerous answers to a generation whose numbers are constantly expanding, and whose access to jobs and education is severely restricted.

Poverty is not the direct cause of the appeal to extremism that can itself lead to terrorism and violence, any more than one could have said "poverty caused Hitler." But poverty, a sense of options closed, of chances and opportunities cut off, is once again dry grass that can lead to conflagration. We have to root out the causes of terrorism as much as we do its awful impact and consequences.

The attack of 9/11 gave rise to the most absurd range of conspiracy theories: it was the act of the U.S. government itself; it must have been caused by Jews because (as the theory goes, in flagrant variance with the facts) no Jews were killed in the World Trade Center. There was the further argument that the United States was "morally responsible" for the attacks because of the oil companies, the U.S. support for Israel, its bases in Saudi Arabia, or whether imperial ambitions could be ascribed to the United States.

The tragedy of 9/11 was, of course, none of these things. It was a deliberate act of violence plotted and planned by Al-Qaeda, whose leader is Osama bin Laden. The violence was directed at civilians, and is rightly described therefore as an act of terror.

The most difficult question for Canadians, as for people throughout the world, is how to respond to the threat of violence, the impact of terrorism?

Some have suggested that "the rules of the game" have changed since 9/11, that key assumptions of the West's legal systems – habeas corpus, the burden of proof – may need to change in the face of the forces of sedition and terrorism.

These are not arguments I can accept. They bear a startling comparison to every argument for the suspension of freedom that has been made since time immemorial. They were the basis for the invasion of Iraq, which has cost tens of thousands of lives, and has not added one jot to the security of the world, in fact, quite the contrary.

Prime Minister Jean Chrétien's wise decision not to support the invasion of Iraq was not taken after reading a poll. It was taken because of the Canadian government's principled view that the invasion was illegal and its pragmatic concern that an invasion can very quickly become an unpopular occupation. These views were wise and correct, although that decision had its critics.

I support Canada carrying its share of difficult burdens, where action is backed by multilateral alliances and due regard is given to supporting peace and reconstruction in the aftermath of conflict.

The United States is Canada's most important bilateral relationship, economically and otherwise, and we should not take that friendship for granted. At the same time, when we have principled disagreements with the Americans, Canada needs to clearly and diplomatically articulate our views. This is expected by Canadians and Americans alike. It is the basis of a sound relationship.

And to speak with our own voice, in the dangerous world we are in, means having our own military capacity. The Canadian Forces are one of the best small militaries in the world, and are recognized around the world as such. They are capable of operating effectively and professionally across the full spectrum – from peacekeeping to combat. Canadians are rightfully proud of this eminent national institution, whose men and women are superb ambassadors for Canada wherever they go in the world. I fully support our troops on whatever mission they are on, and we all grieve as Canadians when they give the ultimate sacrifice.

Security for Canadians is not simply about spending billions on military hardware and doing whatever our neighbour to the south asks on the counter-insurgency front. My experience with Air India and the oversight of CSIS has convinced me that properly supporting CSIS and the RCMP is absolutely essential to the discovery and prevention of terrorist activities in Canada.

So is investing in and promoting values of common citizenship in our schools and communities. Recent experience tells us we need to deepen our dialogue around multiculturalism, diversity, and common citizenship. We can't content ourselves with merely repeating old formulas when isolated pockets of our own citizens somehow feel justified in plotting terror against their fellow Canadians. Our security depends on addressing these issues.

For sixty years, Canada has regarded the United Nations as the key international organization and forum for managing global conflicts. Yet it has become fashionable in conservative circles to be dismissive of the UN.

The UN is far from perfect, and is sorely in need of renewal – but let's remember that 190 countries belong to this organization. No wonder it faces challenges. While not the only multilateral forum, the UN remains the most essential body for managing the major international issues of our time.

We have learned from Iraq that a pre-emptive invasion without a UN mandate, or adherence to international law, will be perceived to lack legitimacy. It risks fomenting rather than calming insurgency. Prime Minister Chrétien's decision to work through the UN to put pressure on Iraq was the right one. He also made the right decision to keep Canada out of that war when the case for invasion was so clearly wanting.

I have written earlier about my experiences in Sri Lanka. At the end of the Second World War, the British colony of Ceylon had a standard of living and literacy rate far ahead of most of its fellow Asian countries. A relatively flourishing and educated country approached independence with a sense of confidence.

Yet there were clouds on the horizon. The postcolonial majority, the Buddhist Sinhala population, felt a strong need to reassert themselves. They felt that the British had favoured the Tamils and insisted that the new country needed to reflect the power of a nationalist generation.

For twenty years the country was locked in a political struggle. Since the early 1970s, it has been immersed in a bitter war. Even the terms used to describe the conflict are politically loaded: "a terrorist insurgency," "a civil war of national liberation," "an ethnic conflict," and on it goes. Sri Lanka's tragedy can be described in numbers: tens of thousands dead; hundreds of thousands made homeless and refugees; billions of dollars in damaged infrastructure; billions more in lost investment.

World attention turned to Sri Lanka after the tsunami in 2004 – horrific coastal flooding that killed thirty thousand people. But little has been said or done about a collapsed ceasefire in the battle between the government of Sri Lanka and the Liberation Tigers of Tamil Eelam (LTTE).

Since January 2006, hundreds of people have been killed. Naval battles, plane strafings, grenade attacks, bombings of buses, markets, and schools. Every day marks a steady increase in violence.

I have visited Sri Lanka several times on behalf of the Forum of Federations, an NGO I served as founding chair for many years. With the exception of Prabhakaran, I have met with the leadership of the country on all sides. It is a place of great beauty, its people caught in the deepest and most complex of tragedies.

There is a growing consensus among outside observers and friends of Sri Lanka, and many within the country, that some kind of federal arrangement needs to be worked out between the parties. For a brief moment, after a meeting in Oslo, in December 2002, it seemed that both the LTTE and the government of Sri Lanka were prepared to explore the federal idea and its application in the country.

But the initial optimism of that apparent agreement soon evaporated. Neither side appears willing to overcome resistance within their own ranks. The political leadership of the Sinhala community is divided and has not made a coherent plan to transcend the communal divide. They can't seem able to come to grips with the compromises and steps forward that are a prerequisite for nation-building.

An internal split within the ranks of the LTTE, the assassination of the Foreign Minister Lakshman Kadirgamar, the failure to use the post-tsunami relief effort as a basis for national reconciliation, have all con-tributed to the schism getting wider, not smaller.

The international community looks on helplessly as the country sinks back into this most difficult and per-sistent of conflicts. Canada and the European Community have now joined the British and the Americans in listing the LTTE as a terrorist organization. Denmark and Sweden are leaving the ceasefire monitoring mission. The death toll is mounting with depressing regularity.

The LTTE is unwilling to make the shift, as did the African National Congress and the Irish Republican Army, from guerilla army to political party. The govern-ment of Sri Lanka is unable to present a plan for a federal constitution that would give important powers and guar-antees to those parts of Sri Lanka that have historically been the homeland of the Tamils.

As we have learned in so many parts of the world, it is one thing to see a solution. It is quite another to get there.

Canada is inevitably affected by the Sri Lankan conflict. People from both sides have now made Canada their home. We should be more engaged than we currently appear to be in helping to create the conditions for peace in this troubled land.

Norway has been playing the role of mediator in this conflict, and Canada has, together with other donor countries, been supportive of their efforts. As a key power in the area, India has also been making an effort to bring an end to the conflict and violence.

Canada should be doing whatever it can to get a peace process back on track.

Conflict resolution should be at the heart of our foreign policy, not an afterthought, or an interesting sideline to other efforts. This will require much greater discipline and determination than we have been able to do so far. We sent a Disaster Assistance Response Team (DART) to the tsunami-ravaged east, we have a few Canadian International Development Agency (CIDA) projects, but nowhere near the clout and focus we should have.

The Canadian Tamil and Sinhala diasporas need themselves to be challenged to overcome the divisions that have been altogether too destructive. The LTTE needs to abandon terrorist tactics. The government of Sri Lanka needs to show a capacity for structural change. Together with others, Canada needs to do what it takes to get the parties to the table.

This brings me to the situation in Afghanistan. The international community was right to overthrow the Taliban – under a UN mandate – because that regime was exporting terrorism. It was right for Canada to have been part of that successful multilateral effort. But we need to keep in mind that Canada's ongoing mission in Afghanistan has changed several times to reflect evolving realities.

In 2002, we sent a battle group to Kandahar; in 2003, we sent two thousand troops to Kabul as part of the NATO-led International Security Assistance Force; in

2004, we reduced this to a seven-hundred-person reconnaissance team; in 2005, we sent a Provincial Reconstruction team to Kandahar. Finally, in early 2006, Canada deployed a combat Task Force to Kandahar and took command of the multinational brigade headquarters.

Paul Martin's government approved the combat component for one year – until early 2007 – to help ensure stability on the ground in Kandahar for reconstruction. But in "jamming" the Canadian Parliament, Stephen Harper has effectively tied up most of Canada's available military resources until 2009 and locked us into a mission geared mainly toward counter-insurgency. There are serious challenges with this.

Canada is in a war, and the questions around this fact have not been given an adequate airing. The rushed six-hour parliamentary debate did not show proper consideration for the complexities of the proposed mission nor for the troops being asked to undertake it.

The responsibility to protect innocent civilians should not be invoked to justify any and all military interventions. Unfortunately, some have appropriated it to rationalize the Iraq War, as well as Canada's involvement in Afghanistan. It does not fit either case. The coalition that invaded Iraq in 2003 did so ostensibly on the pretext of searching for weapons of mass destruction. And the international community intervened in Afghanistan because that country was the source of the 9/11 terrorist attacks.

We need less rhetoric and more realism about Afghanistan. An unpoliced border with northern Pakistan, an economy still deeply dependent on poppy production and the heroin trade, powerful warlords with extensive foreign networks: the notion of a quick military victory and a sudden transition to liberal democracy is problematic. We need to be realistic about what we can achieve, and how long it will take.

There are other options for Canada in Afghanistan between traditional peacekeeping and a largely counter-insurgency role, even if the prime minister does not want to discuss them. Our focus should be on reconstruction, aimed at enabling the Afghan people to provide security within their own borders, and helping them build a legitimate economy.

Doing these things will require much more focus and discipline. It is not about a "wish list" of all the things we like to do or buy. That's not governing. We have to commit the resources we have in a focused way to make them work.

This is the realism that is missing in putting our ideals to work. We need to support the choice of reconstruction, diplomacy, police training, and public institution building with an upgraded diplomatic mission and a major CIDA deployment.

This is also about the role of Parliament. Not just MPs, but also the public should be better and regularly informed. It is difficult for government to do this, but this is an important principle and a new reality. People want to be involved in these policy debates, and government needs to show it is committed to just that.

The Afghan story is a broader lesson of Canada in the world in the twenty-first century. We need clearly defined goals backed by credible resources that are used to acquire the necessary human and material support: diplomats, soldiers, aid workers in sufficient numbers and sufficiently deployed abroad to effectively support our goals and activities, rather than the patchwork system we have in place now. Plus an ongoing dialogue with Canadians about Canada in the world.

Harper has not defined the goals before charging ahead with decisions. His military equipment spending means that he substitutes political opportunism and photo ops for policy. Policy should drive programs, not the other way around.

In foreign deployments, we must maintain a balanced approach and not lose our way as a people committed to diplomacy, aid, reconstruction, and deliberate, responsible decisions when it comes to military action. We should indeed remember who we are.

Canada's long-standing commitment to multilateralism, peacekeeping, and reconstruction is not quaint, romantic, or a sacred cow. Our foreign policy traditions, far from being outmoded, offer an effective framework and a sound set of values for helping stabilize and rebuild in situations of global conflict.

Building sustainable democracies does not come out of the barrel of a foreign gun.

When Lester Pearson argued at the United Nations in 1956 that a peacekeeping mission was essential to counter-act the imperial overreach of Suez, he did not phone Sir Anthony Eden for permission. Nor did Pierre Elliott Trudeau have the enthusiastic support of either superpower when he launched his initiative to point out the folly of the so-called "balance of terror" in the early 1980s.

The notion that in the age of the dominance of the United States we should say "Ready Aye Ready" to whatever lurch comes out of Washington is wrong-headed. It is not anti-American to argue that it is precisely at these moments Canada needs to speak with its own voice.

Canada has on many occasions chosen a different path from the United States. We are by nature multilateral and international in our outlook. We are in the world and the world is in us. We have no Manifest Destiny. We are not an empire, be it heavy or lite. The American constitution is not ours, the circumstances of our "founding" were quite different, and so is who we are and who we can be in the world.

The Air India bombing should have taught us that we are not immune from the violence of the world. The arrests in Toronto in 2006 are yet further confirmation.

We have to be vigilant in defence of our security, and need the deepest and most efficient co-operation between our intelligence services, the RCMP, and local police forces. But Canada also has a Charter of Rights and Freedoms, and the Constitution requires that we remain strong in defence of due process as much as we are vigilant in defence of freedom.

As a country of immigrants, we are home to the world's great religious faiths. We need to do more to ensure that we are all talking to one another, that we do not allow differences to fester, or extremism to grow.

No political issue has been more central to the debate on foreign policy than Israel and the Middle East. Jews from around the world began immigrating in large numbers to what was then Palestine, a colony of the Ottoman Empire, toward the end of the nineteenth century. Jews had, of course, lived in the region since biblical times, but the majority had been dispersed after facing severe persecution. The British took over the imperial role after the First World War and were never able to find the basis for a deep understanding or political settlement between the communities. The demand for the creation of a Jewish state in Palestine took on new life after 1945, and in 1948 Israel was accepted as a member of the United Nations.

Canada has long recognized the right of Israel to live within secure and internationally recognized borders. At the same time, Canada has supported UN resolutions that have sought a full resolution of outstanding issues between all the parties, including the status of Jerusalem and the rights of refugees who left or were displaced in 1948. As the debate has evolved, Canada has fully accepted the need for a two-state solution, in which the rights of Palestinians to their own independent and viable state would be guaranteed, and continues to press for negotiations that would produce an acceptable resolution of differences between all the parties.

With the emergence of more radical groups, like Hamas in Palestine and Hezbollah in Lebanon, and their linkage to states like Iran that refuse to recognize that Israel should be allowed to exist at all, and the deepening of conflict – as seen in the "intifida" and the recent fighting and destruction in Lebanon and northern Israel – the issues are at once more difficult and emotional than ever before. Canada has to remain engaged.

We are not neutral about the outcome of what is happening. A refusal to accept the legitimacy of "the other" lies at the heart of most seemingly irresolvable problems. This is certainly true of the Middle East. Israel has a right to thrive with secure borders. Palestinians have a right to their own country within its own borders. Lebanese people have a right to live in peace and for their government to exercise sovereignty. Terrorism and the targeting of innocent civilians must be resisted.

Radical and fundamentalist religious ideologies are a barrier to peace, to human rights, and even to human survival. Those who cannot accept the presence in the world, or the neighbourhood, of people with different religions, languages, and loyalties are a modern scourge. At their best, they foster ignorance and prejudice. At their worst, they threaten the survival of the human race.

Managing, reducing, and ultimately resolving conflicts in the Middle East is one of the great geopolitical challenges of our time. Canada is not "neutral" about the outcome. Canada must be engaged in helping shape it. The outcome must secure the future of every country in the region: Israel, Lebanon, and Palestine, all as viable, recognized entities with borders that are secure.

These are issues whose resolution will take much time and extraordinary perseverence. A radical Islam that cannot accept pluralism and diversity in the Middle East is an obstacle to an objective that sensible people every-where share.

The question is: How to keep the next generation from embracing these destructive ideologies? A military response to a military provocation is a natural reaction, but any such response, either in Palestinian Authority or Lebanon, always runs the risk of creating more extremists than are being killed. History shows that guerilla groups can abandon terrorism when the political context around them changes. Military firmness has to be matched with the imagination to create that new framework. Every actor in the region has to be as concerned with the consequences of actions as they are with their justification.

The choices we face as a country are not between "decisiveness and dithering" or between "taking sides and neutrality." They are rather between oversimplification and wisdom. We made a choice, the right choice, as a country many years ago when we affirmed our support for an Israeli state in the Middle East. And we also made a wise choice when we affirmed the need for a Palestinian state. Wisdom is about balance, realism, and finding just, enduring solutions. What steps can we take that will ensure real peace, and not just a temporary ceasefire? The answers lie more in the world of politics and diplomacy than they do anywhere else. A military solution on its own won't work.

Canada needs to say "yes" to Israel, Lebanon, and to Palestine, and "no" to terrorism. Canada needs to work with our friends and allies to develop strategies that will have a deep and lasting effect. This is a world where slogans and bumper stickers aren't really effective.

Too many ordinary citizens are being killed, in Haifa, in Tyre, in Qana, in Beirut. We cannot be indifferent to these losses. On the contrary. Canada needs to find its voice again. Canada should be part of the diplomatic effort to devise a plan that gives the Lebanese government the means and support to assert real control of its own territory. A plan that gives all the countries in the region the confidence that the rockets and the cross-border raids will stop. A plan that stops terrorism and the nurturing of terrorism. A plan that once more asserts the need for a resolution of the Palestine issue. Canada must be prepared to commit resources, for reconstruction and effective policing.

A century that gave us unprecedented violence has now been succeeded by a world of bewildering complexity. Simplistic thinking has no place in it. Burke was right – "governing in the name of a theory" is a bad idea. So is invading in the name of a theory. The avoidance of ideological enthusiasm, doing less harm, saving more lives, reconciling differences, eliminating the worst poverty, steadily constructing a world order, step by step, this is the better way of the future.

CONCLUSION

Liberalism speaks to basic values that help define Canada as well as the Liberal Party. Freedom means more than just wanting to be left alone. It is about free speech and association, the right to vote and participate, the right to live in security and not to be deprived of these rights except by due process of law.

For many years, even generations, these rights and values were not entrenched in the Constitution. They were to be protected by Parliament, the legislatures, and the courts based on traditions of common law and legal precedent. Canada's Constitution was for more than a century a piece of British legislation interpreted by the Privy Council in the United Kingdom and, after 1949, the Supreme Court of Canada. The Liberal Party's decision to push for a patriation of the Constitution with an entrenched Charter of Rights and Freedoms was an historic moment in the evolution of the country.

The Charter has come to symbolize Canada. Provincial human-rights legislation provides parallel support for ideas about rights and freedoms, but it is the Charter that provides a framework, the architecture of liberty that is a keystone of Canadian law.

From the beginning, the Charter has had its opponents. I was a member of the House of Commons when it was first presented for debate in 1980. I was, and am to this day, a vigorous supporter of the Charter and what it means for Canada. I believed that minorities would be better protected, that women's equality struggles would be enhanced, and that a creative dialogue between the courts and Parliament could be established.

Some argued that the courts, as inherently conservative institutions, would inevitably side with the interests of money and property. Others objected that the Charter would override provincial jurisdictions and make life too difficult for bureaucrats and administrators across the country. There will always be arguments about individual court decisions and judgments. But on balance (that word again), the Charter has served us well. Aboriginal rights have been advanced, as the rule of law has been rightly extended. The Supreme Court has insisted that Parliament take seriously its own legislation on equal pay, and has given teeth to concepts of freedom of association and due process before the law.

The Conservatives have responded to this with cries of "judicial activism," and have gone out of their way to denounce court decisions on Aboriginal rights, abortion, and anything else that disturbs their sense of what's Right in the world. If Stephen Harper and his friends had their way, there would never have been a Charter. The architecture of liberty that the Supreme Court has helped define would never have been built. As the Conservatives reassert themselves, the attacks on the Supreme Court and the politicization of justice and the Constitution that is such a feature of American politics will emerge in Canada as well. They will import that approach, along with attacks on environmentalists, advocates of women's rights, and the constitutional protection of gay and lesbian rights.

It is ironic that it is so-called conservatives who have become so uncomfortable with the rule of law. Falling back on the mantra that "judges should interpret the law, not make it," they fail to remember that it is the independence of the judiciary, not its submissiveness, that lies at the heart of our Constitution. Judicial discretion is not something to be applauded only when the decision is favourable to one side or the other. It is about something much more profound – that while Parliament can make laws, it is the judges' responsibility to exercise their best wisdom in applying and interpreting those same laws.

Nor is this an issue that started with the Charter.

Whether it was Alberta's notorious proposed Press Law, or Quebec's Padlock Law, a pre-Charter court made it clear that legislatures could not flout the basic principles of our constitutional life – freedom of speech, freedom of association, and due process. Political enthusiasm led Maurice Duplessis to believe that he could deny the granting of a liquor licence to a restaurant owner on the grounds that he was a supporter of the Jehovah's Witnesses. The Supreme Court of Canada told Premier Duplessis he was wrong, that he was duty bound to be fair, twenty-five years before the Charter.

Bora Laskin, Canada's great chief justice of the 1970s, asserted basic principles of equity in recognizing the value of a spouse's contribution to the family farm in a famous divorce case. These were then adopted by legislatures across the country in their family law statutes. My point here is that modern liberalism (and Liberalism) stands foursquare behind the due process of law. The Charter is the clearest codification of that principle. But the Charter did not create it. It simply expressed it.

One of the main features of the debate before and after the Charter has been its protection of due process. The Supreme Court of the United States under the leadership of Chief Justice Earl Warren provided clear rules insisting that evidence be collected properly, that suspects be "read their rights," and that the protection of due process had to be applied to those suspected of a criminal offence.

These protections gave rise to a considerable reaction, with the inevitable view that "the hands of the police are being tied," and that "the law cares more about the criminal than it does about the victim." The Charter's protections have, over the past twenty-five years, been applied to those charged with criminal offences, and a similar debate has unfolded in Canada.

The Harper Conservatives have made a particular point of insisting that they would lead a government that would be tougher on crime and criminals than any of its Liberal predecessors. Minimum sentences, moving the age of full criminal responsibility to sixteen and potential criminal liability to ten (who says they don't have a child-care policy?), and generally raising the rhetorical decibel level on "getting tough on bad guys" has been the order of the day.

The public's right to security, to be able to live free of crime and harassment, to have property protected and secured are values that Canadians take seriously. Peace, order, and good government are core values of the Canadian Constitution precisely because they reflect the desire we all have to live in a society where civility and order are respected by government and the courts.

Criminality is not on the rampage in Canada. However, if your home has been invaded, your car stolen, or you are the victim of violent crime, statistical reassurance has no real meaning.

As the population ages, the amount of crime generally goes down. At the same time, an older public becomes more afraid of violent attack or property theft. As Liberals, we need to take those concerns seriously. We also need to engage the public in a discussion about what needs to be done.

The Liberal approach needs to follow the straightforward philosophy of "tough on crime, tough on the causes of crime." All Canadians want their political leaders to take crime seriously. But what should distinguish Liberals is our insistence that we deal with the underlying social and economic conditions that allow crime to thrive.

We also need to do a better job of listening to police and others about their actual experience in fighting crime, and the difficulties they encounter. Few Canadians understand how the demands for due process affect the daily tasks of policing. Getting a conviction for drunk driving requires a painstaking attention to detail that is time-consuming and difficult. There is a difference between passing a law and implementing it, and some of the frustrations of front-line officers can be traced to the lack of understanding about the difficulties they face on a daily basis.

No area of public policy is so full of sloganeering. Minimum sentences will fill jails and increase provincial budgets. Will they reduce crime? There is no international evidence that would support such a conclusion, but there is also no denying the public's frustration with repeat offenders and the perception of revolving-door justice.

In the Canadian system, the federal government is responsible for the Criminal Code. The provinces and municipalities pay for policing and the administration of justice. So this is an area where real dialogue and cooperation are critical. Firewalls will be no help here.

We also need to have a candid discussion about how certain groups are substantially over-represented in the criminal population. Men under the age of thirty, and Aboriginal and afro-Canadians in particular, are more likely to be convicted and in jail. It does no good to hide these facts. Indeed, we can't begin to get tougher on the causes of crime until we face life as it is lived. Programs that take families, neighbourhoods, schools, and jobs seriously have to be at the centre, not the fringes, of public policy. Crime prevention strategies developed with and by affected communities can make a real difference. Opportunities for youth, including recreation, training, employment, the sense that a community cares about their futures – these things are as important as visible and effective police responses to crime. And making very clear that breaking the law has consequences with a real price attached.

Fighting crime is too important to be left to the Conservatives. Their views on what needs to be done are simplistic and disjointed. Their model and rhetoric, in this as in so much else, is the Republican United States, which has probably the least successful crime and jail strategy in the Western world.

The Tories have been silent lately on the return of the death penalty. A new parliamentary vote on this subject is virtually inevitable given the enthusiasm of a number of their members on this subject. The death penalty, we know, does not reduce crime. It does not deter criminals. Its use in the United States has resulted in the execution of many who were not guilty of the offence. This does not slow the determination of the Harper right, but it should give profound pause to the rest of us.

I am opposed to the return of the death penalty in Canada. It cheapens life. It makes the state a killer. It doesn't deter crime or stop the criminal. It means innocent people will be executed for crimes they didn't commit.

If "getting tough on crime" is one conservative mantra, "family values" is another. One of the key sources of political success of the right in the United States and elsewhere has been their effort to capture language and symbols that resonate with the public. "Law and order" was the phrase of the 1970s.

Liberals need to be careful not to let Conservatives run with these issues without getting called on them. The modern family is a diverse place – our hearts should be big enough to embrace all of them, not just the *Father Knows Best* model that dominates Conservative rhetoric. Women's equality, full civic recognition for gays and lesbians – these are not threats to family values. They are a recognition that equality and a full acceptance of people as they really are lie at the heart of a free and caring society.

Of course, this represents an evolution in thinking. A hundred years ago, women's inferiority in political matters was widely accepted, and homosexuality was seen as a form of deviant and dangerous behaviour that was to be repressed.

But times have changed, people's consciousness has changed, and our understanding of human rights has changed as well. The great strength of liberalism is its acceptance of change, its ability to embrace the future. The Conservatives have difficulty with change, difficulty with dealing with the future unless it can be exactly like the past. Fortunately, the Charter of Rights and Freedoms, and the Supreme Court's insistence on giving the Charter meaning, now prevent the Conservatives from imposing their views on everyone else.

Churches, synagogues, and mosques are, of course, free to insist on whatever doctrinal practice they want within their own jurisdiction. But the state's sphere must also be protected, and that means recognizing that gay and lesbian couples are legally entitled to marry.

The Liberal Party was right to become the party of the Charter. It has helped to focus our attention on the rights of the vulnerable and disadvantaged.

To govern is to choose. This is the hardest lesson of politics. And, often as not, the choice is not between good and bad, or between easy and difficult. Laurier knew that when he made his most difficult choice. A wartime Cabinet post seemed to many the best path. He refused to take it, knowing it would open him to the charge of being "soft on war" when young Canadian men were dying in the thousands. He did so, fighting and losing an election in 1917, because he was determined to keep the country together, and knew that with the passage of time a principled position would be understood as the wiser choice.

Pearson knew it when he challenged the prevailing orthodoxy of the British and French foreign offices and crafted a peaceful resolution of the Suez Crisis. It did not win him instant popularity in Canada. John Diefenbaker won what was then the greatest majority in Canadian history in 1958.

Pierre Trudeau knew it when he held firm on the principle of an entrenched Charter of Rights and Freedoms. He compromised to get it, but the principle won out.

We like to think of ourselves as a peaceable kingdom, whose history, as the saying goes, is as dull as ditchwater and whose politicians are full of it. Yet conflict and its resolution have been an indelible part of our story.

The morality of federalism triumphed over other visions because it alone allowed different people and groups to live together without submerging their own identity. The Supreme Court of Canada put it this way in its landmark unanimous opinion on secession:

"a thousand strands of accommodation make a nation."

Nor should anyone think that these acts of accommodation are signs of weakness. This kind of active celebration of diversity, this recognition of difference, this acknowledgment of the integrity of "the other" – all these imply a rejection of something else: a view that my beliefs, my "one Canadianness" should prevail.

Nor do we have to define ourselves by what we are not: our self-definition includes that we are North Americans, that we share a continent with others who are at once more populous and powerful than we are. Anti-Americanism, with its roots going back to the very formation of our country, is too limiting, too narrow, too insecure to really reflect who we are today. We are alike and we are different, and we are confident in our difference. We shouldn't be preoccupied with proving either.

Lester Pearson knew that when he insisted on Canada retaining an independent perspective on both the Middle East and Vietnam. He knew it when he crafted the Canada Pension Plan and the framework for our national health-care system.

Pierre Trudeau and Jean Chrétien each knew it as they kept Canada on the sound path of a sovereign foreign policy as the basis of their approach to politics. Canadians want a voice, not an echo. At its best, it is a firm voice, not a strident one.

The country's commitment to diversity should not be confused with a reluctance to insist on shared values. Far more than the Parliament and premiers who supported it at the time realized, the Charter of Rights and Freedoms expresses these values. Due process, respect for the judiciary, democracy, equality before the law, pluralism, the recognition of diversity: at key points, both Parliament and the courts have gone out of their way to reassert the common values that matter.

And then there is the land. We love Canada for its people and for the communities we have built – just as we should lament the urban sprawl, global warming, and the degradation of our water and air that have accompanied our prosperity. Yet Murray McLauchlan is right when he sings that the soul of the country is north of the timberline. Our sense of a vast geography and an untrammelled wilderness is deeply part of who we are.

A Canadian is anyone who loves this land and its people and has chosen to make it home. Period. There is no "Un-Canadian Affairs Committee" of the House of Commons. There are two official languages, dozens of languages and dialects indigenous to the land, and hundreds more spoken in families, on street corners, and in churches, temples, synagogues, and mosques.

The diversity of opinion expressed in these places could only threaten the security and civility of Canada if people forget the underlying values we share as citizens.

The strength of Canadian liberalism is that at its heart it has consistently expressed core values that have helped to define the country. From the commitment to public education and responsible government of the pure grits of Ontario and Joseph Howe of Nova Scotia to the resolute commitment to secular democracy of the nineteenth-century Rouges, to today's commitment to the Charter, the rule of law, and the need to balance unity and diversity, the Liberal Party has expressed values that speak to the heart of the country.

When Laurier talked of "Canada first, Canada last, Canada always," he was speaking to an emergent nationalism that wanted a country to be itself, not just an offshoot of Empire. We need that spirit to be reborn and reasserted as we watch Stephen Harper's conservatism try to take us elsewhere.

There are those who are happy if Canada becomes a willing follower of another empire. I am not among them. I want Canada to be itself, as well as to understand that we cannot be just for ourselves. We owe one another, we owe generations to come, more and better than this. That is why I say Canada is "in the balance."

We can choose a widely shared prosperity based on understanding the role of learning and innovation in the global economy, or simplistic policy choices based on shallow calculations. We can join together in building on our past successes in welfare and social services, or we can see them erode in a rush to imitate those societies that have allowed the ties of mutual support to become frayed to a point where they can't be recognized.

We can continue to embrace the Canada of the Charter, where human rights are taken seriously, where equality between women and men is celebrated and protected, where gays and lesbians can be themselves openly, and their marriages can be recognized, where Aboriginal rights are advanced by courts and championed by legislatures and Parliaments, or we can have a

Canada where the judiciary is attacked, the Charter is ignored, and fundamental rights of Aboriginal people, gays and lesbians, and minorities are subject to constant challenge and even ridicule. We can join others in the world who are ready to change their approach to production and pollution, and thus keep climate change under control, or we can fuel the forces in denial, and thereby ensure a world that is hotter, more polluted, and far more precarious.

The Liberal Party helped build the foundations of Canadian nationhood, and in Laurier found a leader who could express the deep desire to fashion a common citizenship north of the forty-ninth parallel.

In King, St. Laurent, Pearson, and Trudeau, we found leaders who kept the country whole, allowed the federal government to evolve as the guardian of the prosperity and well-being of the Canadian people, and expanded further the scope of Canadian sovereignty.

John Turner fought valiantly for an independent Canada. Jean Chrétien and Paul Martin inherited the most difficult of economic situations, and succeeded in creating fiscal discipline and renewed social investment. The decision to say no to George Bush's war and keep Canada's troops out of Iraq was wise and courageous.

When I was a kid, one of my favourite TV shows was Rod Serling's *The Twilight Zone.* I remember one episode where the passengers in a plane come through the sky only to discover that on their flight they've gone back in time dramatically. On their first attempt at landing, there are dinosaurs roaming around, on the second it looks like the nineteenth century. On their third and final attempt, the pilot tells them that the best he can do is about 1940.

That *Twilight Zone* episode reminds me of the Harper government. They don't have a vision of Canada that lets them get to Canada as it is, let alone as it could be.

The future of Canada is indeed in the balance. What happens will depend very much on the choices we make. But, "in the balance" means something else as well. The best public policy is, from my experience, very much about balance, about breaking through complexity, understanding that not everything is one-sided. We need to regain that balance as well.

It will require leadership and courage to work with Canadians in making the choices that best reflect our values and our interests. We have found those qualities in the past. We shall find them again in the future.